Both Sides of the Bars

Anthony Bryant

To: Dr. Mark Smith
Great meeting you and looking forward to
future partnerships

Bailey Publishing

Blessings

Anthony Bryant

4/20/21

BOTH SIDES OF THE BARS
By Antony Bryant

Co-written by Patty Jo Sawvel
Kernersville, North Carolina

Published by Bailey Press, a division of
Classic Writing and Public Relations
Kernersville, North Carolina
www.ClassicWritingPR.com

ISNB 978-1537530376

Cover Designer: Robyn Washington Cox
Greensboro, North Carolina

Illustrations by Raiden Hiatt

For more information visit the author's website:
www.split2nd.weebly.com

Dedication

My children—Tranise and Anthony Jr.

Despite my absence during the vast majority of your childhood, you have defied the odds, and have conquered the negative statistics and stereotypes that oftentimes are associated with children growing up without a father. Thank you for your continual love and respect.

My Mother—Marilyn Bryant

Although you are no longer here on earth with us, your spirit will remain in my heart forever. You are a true Proverbs 31 woman. I am blessed to have you as my mom, and to have experienced the impact you've made in my life.

All forms of Law Enforcement, Corrections & Probation Officers

Your job can be demanding, stressful, and oftentimes thankless in the eyes of society. The temptations and peer pressures can be overwhelming at times. Thank you for what you do each day and for doing what is right.

Special Acknowledgements

My cheerleaders helped me in so many ways to make this book a reality. Pictured with me: Joe and Gladys Grimaud, Leon Cureton, Greg and Rhonda Sue Lyman, Ken and Helen McDougal, Dan and Gwen Potts, Victoria Mokeba, Dennis and Beverly Pinnell. Not pictured: Samuel Mokeba, Pearlie Cureton, Steve and Candice Scutt, David and Kaye Dixon and Kyle and Jamie Himmelwright.

My Former Wife and Mother of My Two Children—
Meeting you at the young age of fifteen years, was one of the
best blessings of my life. Everything I accomplished during our
12 years of marriage, I owe to a mature, strong woman who
knew how to mold a teenager into a man. I could not have asked
for a better mother for our children. Much respect and blessings
to you for the indelible impact you've had in my life.

Joe & Gladys Grimaud—Without a doubt, our connection
was clearly and divinely orchestrated by God. I met you less
than 90 days after my release and would not be where I am today
had it not been for your love, prayers, support, encouragement,
guidance and advice. You continue to direct me through life with
wisdom as only a parent would do, and for that reason, I am
eternally grateful.

Tanika Bryant—Not only my little sister, but my biggest cheer
leader and encourager. You've been with me since day one,
during almost eleven years of my valley season, and afterwards.
Your prayers, letters, words of encouragement, visits and
financial support truly made the difference. You made life
bearable behind the bars.

Tommie Simpson Osborne—My friend and former partner,
both at the Chatham County Sheriff's Department as a
Corrections Officer and the Chatham County Police Department
as a Police Officer. You did it right—balancing your family and
your career—while staying well inside the line of ethics. Thank
you for being a positive role model.

Steve Pickens—My best friend in elementary school. Thanks for your friendship despite the racial, social/economic differences that separated most people during the 70's.

Many Pastors—Paul Johnson, Brad Bellomy, Dennis Pinnell, Kyle Himmelwright, and Nazarene South Carolina District Superintendent, Dr. Eddie Estep. Thank you for your profound impact in my spiritual growth and development as a leader and preacher of the gospel. Pastor Redfern, thanks for your friendship, insight and encouragement to write this book.

Dana & Eva Marsee—Although we have not met in person as yet, I remember the first letter that I received from you back in 1999, while housed at the Lexington Kentucky Federal Prison. Throughout the years, you have been there encouraging and praying with me via telephone and letters. We have remained friends to this day and looking forward to meeting you in person. Thank you for all the love and support you've given me.

Angela Green—For your friendship, visits, letters, phone conversations, and prayers during my valley season and afterwards.

Willie Padget—My first cousin and friend. Thanks for the website design, words of encouragement, prayers, and believing in me.

Christina Smith Galloway—For your friendship and help by capturing my image in the orange jumpsuit and my bow tie.

Patty Jo Sawvel—My writer. You pulled memories out of me that I'd long forgotten. Thank you for your never-ending questions and insistence on double-checking the facts. Your expertise and knowledge were priceless. I contracted with you for business, but you became my friend.

Stephanie Smith—For your support, prayers, encouragement and marketing.

Additional Acknowledgements

My Dad—Tommy Bryant Sr., Tony Parker, Pastor Stan, Kelly Simmons, Pastor Sweatman. My siblings—Tommy Jr., Irvin, Sharon, Tanika, Marvin, Ramone and Shantel. Pastor Kendricks, Alston Wilkes Society, Mac & Marianne McGee, Sumona Brown. My Nazarene church family and friends. Pastor Sylvia, Dr. David and Kaye Nixon, Dr. A.V. Strong, Pastor Coleman, Terry Dozier, Jerlene Baldwin, Henry Simons, Doug & Demestress Williams, Pastor Ricky Temple, Dr. Carlos & Alana Staley, Pastor Sammy Wade, Stacey Bullard, Brent Peterson, Henry Flowers, Brad & Krista Bellomy, Pastors Lee & Jennette Haynes, and Carl & Katrina Fox.

Contents

Chapter One

You Are Under Arrest

It was about 3 o'clock in the morning. My wife, Red, and I were sound asleep, along with our two children.

Suddenly I heard, "Knock, knock, knock, knock, knock, knock," on the front door. It may as well have been six rifle shots—the way it jolted every nerve in my body. My eyes flew open and my limbs stiffened, but I didn't get up. I lay there in a quiet panic.

"This is it," I thought silently. "I stopped doing wrong a year ago, figured that I'd buried it and here it is. Who found out my secret? Had the other guys been caught? Or, was it a police investigation?"

"Knock, knock, knock, knock, knock, knock." The banging came again.

This time, Red said a bit impatiently, "Anthony, you gonna get that?"

After all, I was a police officer. At 3 o'clock in the morning, there are only two types of people that knock on your door like that. It's either a very bold robber or the police.

Without a word, I got up, slipped on some shorts, and walked slowly to the door. I swear it was like walking the Green Mile. I was scared. Horrified. The most scared I'd ever been in my life.

For a moment, I thought about running, but quickly erased that option—knowing that police always case the perimeter of a house in an arrest of this magnitude. Also, I didn't want to leave Red and the children in harm's way.

1

As I approached the door, I yelled, "Who is it!" My heart was pounding and my throat felt like I hadn't had a drink of water for a year.

Then a voice returned, "Anthony, open the door. I'm here with agents from the FBI."

I opened the door and realized that my worst nightmare had now become a reality. I thought to myself, "My whole world is about to crumble. I just don't know how."

Standing on my porch were two officers from my department. One was Major Billy Freeman, a high-ranking major, and the other was Officer Willie Phillips, who'd recently been promoted to detective. Beside them were two FBI agents.

I could barely utter the words, "Come in."

Major Freeman said matter-of-factly, "We have a warrant for your arrest for attempt to aid and abet the distribution of cocaine."

Next, one of the FBI officers said, "We have video evidence to prove your involvement…"

As he was talking, my 11-year-old daughter peeked her head around the corner and caught my eye. My wife, who was holding back in the hallway, told her sternly, "Get back to your room!"

Then, my wife came out and asked, "Anthony, what's going on?"

She had no idea what I'd been up to. I played the innocent role the whole time the officers were in our house to make it easier on her and the children.

"Baby," I said, "They say that they have video tapes of me doing something wrong and as a result, I'm being arrested. So, I'm going to go with them to look at the video and see what they are talking about."

Red stood there in disbelief—totally stunned. I think the officers from my department were equally shocked by this whole arrest because I had an excellent reputation as an officer. In fact, I was about to be promoted.

Suddenly I heard an officer ask me, "Where is your gun and your keys?"

"My weapon is in my bedroom, in the closet on the top shelf, and my keys are on my dresser," I said directly.

Detective Willie Phillips went to retrieve the items while the other officer handed me a blue jumpsuit. As I slipped out of my shorts, I realized that I was stepping out of my life as a father, husband, and police officer, and into the life of an inmate.

In that moment of truth, I felt a profound sense of loss—not for my career as a police officer—but for my role as a father who could speak into the lives of his children. I wasn't sure how long I'd be going to prison. Maybe five years. But, that would put my daughter at the age of 16—beyond the most memorable years of her childhood—and my son at the age of nine, before I would be released.

Right on the heels of that loss was the devastation I felt at the death of my career. In my two short years with the Chatham County Police Department, being a sworn officer had clearly become more than a job. It was my identity.

Sadly, the least of my losses was that of my loyal and supportive wife, Red. Early into my new career, I'd marginalized my relationship with her and nearly everyone else in my life to bond with the "brotherhood" of fellow officers. The things we did to bond and build trust with each other broke trust with our wives and families. So, our relationship was already on the edge when this deal breaker happened.

The officer said politely, "I'm going to have to put handcuffs on you."

I turned around and tuned into the moment. As he carefully clicked the cuffs, I realized that he didn't want to be doing this. It went against every fiber of his being to be arresting Anthony Bryant—a model officer with excellent citations from both the community and the department. But he did his job—all four of them actually—with a high level of dignity and respect for me.

Then, one officer took each arm, and led me out the front door and down to the police car. The only thing I could say to Red was, "I'm sorry. I'm sorry. I'm sorry."

As we rode away, I looked out the window. Tears welled up in my eyes as I watched my home, my family, and my life as I knew it quickly disappear.

I marked the date. Wednesday, September 10, 1997. Later, I found out that I was one of 11 police officers arrested in Savannah, Georgia. We were snagged in one of the most successful FBI stings to date.

Turning inward, I wondered, "What did I ever do to get myself into this situation?"

Chapter Two
Examining the Foundation

To understand "why" I made that fatal split-second decision to engage in illegal activity, I had to retrace my life clear down to the roots of my beginning. I was born into the family tree of Marilyn "Betty" Hamilton Bryant, a God-fearing, kindhearted, church-going Christian and Tommy Bryant, Sr., a rugged, hard-working, hard-drinking, and sometimes pot-smoking truck driver, who happened to be the son of a preacher.

In my early childhood—from my birth as the second son on September 4, 1967—until 1975, just before the birth of my parent's fifth child, we lived in subsidized apartments at 628 Fellwood Homes.

We lived with the poorest of the poor—mainly all black families, but with a few poor whites sprinkled in. The apartments were so run down that our battle with cockroaches and mice was constant. I remember every night before we went to bed, we would set spring-loaded mouse traps in the kitchen. Before we even got up the stairs and into our beds, we would hear, "Pop, pop, pop, pop, pop." Sure enough, in the morning we'd have four or five dead mice.

Mom kept us fairly close to home. We only wandered a house or two away. Mainly, we played in a small clearing in front of our house. Though we played ball, chase, and other childhood games, there was a prevailing sense of tension in the neighborhood.

For entertainment, sometimes I'd sneak upstairs out of the hot Savannah sun to watch the neighbors across the street. The woman would curse the man and then the man would get up in her face. They pushed and shoved in an angry, but predictable, dance. I watched intently, wondering what would happen next, because stuff like that never happened at my house.

Suddenly, I would hear mom call, "Anthony, are you up there looking out your window? You get yourself down here right now!"

Even though we lived in one of the poorest neighborhoods, for some reason, I was selected to be bused to the predominately white school—Windsor Forest Elementary School. The school was as stately as its name, and I liked it.

I noticed that I was one of only six black children surrounded by about 18 white children in my class. This was very different from my nearly all black neighborhood. But, I didn't see color as a problem. Mama always taught us to treat everyone the same, and everyone here seemed to like me.

Part of what helped ease the transition is that I liked to have fun—like most elementary school boys—and I had a pretty good sense of humor. Then, in second grade, Steve Pickens and I became best friends.

His dad came into school one day to show and tell what it is like to do his job. After the presentation, Steve ran up to his dad and said, "Dad, this is Anthony, my best friend."

His dad said with a big grin, "Oh, I've heard a lot about you, Anthony."

He hugged me and made me feel like family. This was so different from the way I was treated just a couple of years earlier when I went to the Kress five and dime store with my mom. When we went in, she sat on a stool at the counter and while she was ordering, I decided to sit in one of the nice booths. When she saw my little black bottom in the "whites only" section, she about had a heart attack!

She snatched me out of that seat quicker than a firefighter saving a child in a burning building. I turned my four-year-old eyes upward and asked, "Mama, why can't we sit in the booth instead of these hard stools?" She didn't exactly answer me, but my father did.

My dad didn't directly comment on this incident. But, he was always complaining about how the white "crackers" took all the best things in life. Particularly, they took the high paying truck routes and left the black drivers with the leftovers—the nickel and dime work. Daddy didn't trust white people and he sure didn't like them.

Ultimately, I sided with Mama. God made all colors of people and it was my job to treat everyone kindly. Besides, it was clear to me that Steve and his grown-up father honestly liked me. Undeniable proof of their acceptance came when Steve celebrated his seventh birthday. He invited me to his birthday party!

Steve Pickens, the little guy in the suit, and I were best friends in school.

His parents drove to the housing projects to pick me up so that I could attend Steve's 7th birthday party.

The day of the party, a big station wagon pulled up to our apartment. Mama exchanged quick and kind greetings with the driver and we were off. As the car full of children headed toward Steve's subdivision, it was as if I was driving into a whole new world. Everyone had huge green lawns and as we drove by, they waved at us. They were actually happy to see us.

I reflected on how different this was from my neighborhood. When we drove up to our house, people stood in the road as if to say, "What do you want? Why you bothering me?" It seemed like no one ever waved, but they sure did fight a lot.

As we got closer to Steve's house—passing one beautiful home after another—a prevailing sense of peace came over me. I never knew people—white or black or any color—lived like this. I liked it.

In Steve's house, my toes sunk into thick chocolate brown carpet. The furniture was all so beautiful—it all matched. And, the living room was as big as our entire apartment.

The birthday party was fun, too. I knew most of the fellas, because we were all in the same class. Steve's parents generously provided the traditional fare with cake, games, and the "Happy Birthday" song. But mostly, I remember the peace and acceptance. Even though I was the only black child at the party—everyone treated me like family.

Thankfully, the summer before I turned eight, my parents moved to 1900 Westlake Avenue, apartment #68. While it was still government subsidized, it had the spirit of the Windsor Forest neighborhood. Here, people treated people like family. It seemed like we were one giant black family. We went inside one another's houses to get drinks of water and moms hugged all the kids.

It was here that Mama started a little snack store, right inside of our four bedroom apartment. She bought bulk items, such as giant dill pickles and potato chips. Then, she made single servings in baggies to sell for 25 or 30 cents. She bought all our favorite candies—Blow Pops, Chick-O-Sticks, Bit-O-Honey, and Now & Later taffy—and sold them at a small profit. Plus, Mama made "thrills"—handmade popsicles—using Kool-Aid, a cup, and a popsicle stick. Neighborhood kids were happy to pay 10 cents for one of these cool treats during the hot summer.

Mama used this money to buy extras for her family, which eventually came to include eight children. She also used this as a way to get to know virtually everyone in our 100-unit complex. She became—in a sense—one of the mothers of the community. She was always home, always kind, and always dependable.

Both Sides of the Bars

Chapter Three

Big Brother

Next to my parents, my older brother, Tommy Bryant, Jr., had the most significant influence in my life. Just three years older than me, Tommy was the ultimate big brother.

He taught me how to navigate my relationship with my father in my early years. Though dad was not home daily, when he was there, he was extremely strict. He would do "surprise inspections" of our closets and our beds. If they were not "ship shape," we would be whipped severely.

I remember one time dad was teaching me to make my bed. He pulled the covers up, smoothed them, made crisp corners, and squared the pillow. He repeated the process several times—which in itself, tried his patience.

After about the fifth consecutive lesson, he asked me, "Got it?"

"Yes Sir," I replied.

The next day he checked my bed. I didn't have it, but I got it. I got about 10 whacks with his leather belt, so much so that it drew welts on my body.

So, Tommy took a lot of time teaching me to make my bed properly. He didn't make my bed for me, but he patiently stuck by my side as he closely examined for wrinkles and sloppy corners.

He'd say encouragingly, "You've got to do better than this, Anthony. Dad will get you for that."

Then he would show me the right way. I was a bit of a slow learner, but for some reason, Tommy took mercy on me. It hurt him to see dad whip me.

Probably one of the reasons he cared for me was because I was a little runt. Not like him—a boy built strong for his age. I was always on the tiny side—small boned and thinly muscled. I think he felt a bit sorry for me.

Dad was also obsessed with the proper way to hang shirts and pants on hangers. Shirts were pretty easy. Make sure the top button was closed and the shoulders rested squarely on the ends of the hanger. Pants were much more frustrating.

To pass the "Dad" inspection, both creases had to be lined up on the pant legs.

Tommy would say, "Okay, Anthony, you got your pants to stay on the hanger, but look at this crease over here. It's not lined up."

I would go to pull the pant leg over a bit and the whole thing would slide off the hanger. Tommy would patiently pick it up and show me again.

"Try lining your pant legs up on the bed and then gently sliding your hanger under your pants," Tommy coached.

Sometimes this worked fine, but sometimes the hanger would drag on my bedspread and then jerk my pants out of line. It was a constant battle for me and I wondered, "How long does a boy have to spend trying to hang his pants on a hanger?" I had more important things to do. My friends were calling me out to play.

We also had daily chores, which once assigned were yours until you found a paying job. My chore was the bathroom—military style. My dad didn't believe in 8 year olds doing an 8-year-old job. He believed in learning it right and doing it right.

Right in the bathroom meant that every surface was washed down. We went way beyond the bowl and the seat. We washed the toilet all the way down to the bolts. And it was the same way for the rest of the bathroom. Dad never wanted to hear the words, "But I did it." All that Dad wanted was to see a squeaky-clean bathroom with no excuses. Big brother Tommy helped me out with this too.

As we grew older, Tommy became popular with the girls and well-respected by the guys. He used his influence to pave the way for me and to protect me.

One time, when I was about 14, I was shooting hoops with Eric Green. Now, Eric was only three months older than me, but we were at completely opposite ends of the growth spectrum. In fact, he grew up to be so big and strong that he was selected by the Pittsburgh Steelers in the 1st round of the 1990 NFL draft.

On this occasion, I had the ball and he wanted it.

"Give me the ball," he demanded.

"It's my ball," I defended.

When I refused to be verbally bullied, he thrust out his oversized hand over my face like a facemask and pushed me to the ground. I started crying, not because I was hurt, but because I was humiliated. Eric made me feel powerless.

He knew he was out of line and a few minutes later, we patched things up and we were playing again. But someone got word to Tommy that Big Eric was bullying his kid brother. Before I knew it, Tommy was on the court challenging Eric.

"You wanna pick on someone, Eric? Don't pick on someone smaller than you. Pick on someone your own size," Tommy said angrily.

Eric said nothing.

"You wanna pick on me? Come on! I'm your size," he dared Eric.

Eric just stood there silently. He and Tommy may have been the same size, but Tommy had been working his muscles with iron weights for two years longer than Eric. There was no contest.

"Yeah," Tommy said cockily. "You just remember this. Don't be bothering Anthony or you'll be dealing with me."

Wow. I felt good. How many people have a big brother that will stand up for them like that! In this case, it wasn't necessary because the group of guys I hung with always settled their differences and got back to the game within a few minutes.

It wasn't like today where someone might go home and get a gun. That never happened in my neighborhood. Still, it was nice to know that Tommy cared enough to stop what he was doing to defend his younger brother.

That fall, when I started high school, Tommy let me hang out with him and his buddies. By then, he'd been working for a couple of years. He had a car, was a drummer, and dressed really nice. When he and the upperclassmen went out to eat, Tommy took me along and paid my way.

I know this was not due to my own merits. Traditionally, the older crowd shuns the newbies. But Tommy blazed a path for me. I was riding on Tommy's shirttail and he let me.

In fact, when he graduated from high school, he bequeathed me his favorite "lucky" shirt. It was a Colours brand baby-blue and white striped Oxford tuck in shirt. He wore it tails out and had the build to model it nicely. I was small, skinny, and a bit of a neat freak, so I tucked it in. But any way that I wore it—it reminded everyone that I was Tommy's brother and I was all right.

With Dad away so much, Tommy sometimes had to step in as a part-time father figure. He let me know when I was doing wrong, but he did it respectfully. I always took his advice because I knew that he had my best interest at heart. He was all about making things better for the family.

As we grew into adults, I continued to follow Tommy. I built an ever-stronger bond of loyalty, trust, and even a sense of obligation toward him. In time, his influence on my life loomed larger than that of my parents, God, or anyone else.

Both Sides of the Bars

Chapter Four

Middle School

School for me was a social event. I went to school to have fun and there was plenty of fun to be had. When I arrived at middle school, my values shifted slightly. I discovered girls, fashion, and sports.

No one wants to be isolated in middle school, so I worked hard to be the "cool guy" that everyone wanted to eat lunch with. Once again, my well-honed sense of humor helped. But that wasn't enough for middle school. I needed nice clothes—some of which were passed down from Tommy—and a sport so that I could watch those beautiful cheerleaders.

So in 7th grade, I started playing basketball for the YMCA and the Frank Callen Boys Club. The coaches really liked my quick response and high energy. Plus, I was a left-handed point guard which was difficult to defend.

Though I didn't really know it at the time, being on a team helped me learn to deal with disappointments—like losses and injuries. It helped me connect the dots between working for a goal and achieving a goal. But mostly, at a critical time in my life, it taught me to focus on something bigger than myself—the team.

By eighth-grade, I was pretty confident in myself. I'd found my place, not only on the basketball court, but also on the dance floor. I used to watch the latest dance moves on television and then practice and practice until I had them down to the tiniest detail.

My dad used to get a big kick out of this. He'd be surrounded with his drinking buddies and call me over.

"Hey Anthony. Show the guys that new dance you learned," he'd say with a laugh.

"What you call that thing?" he'd ask.

"The Pop N Lock," I'd say with a grin.

"Show us how it's done."

I'd flip on the music and command my body to move to the beat. Some of my moves were as crisp and predictable as a robot and then my body would suddenly go limp. My head was going one way and my hips the other as I glided across the floor. Done right, it looked unreal. Almost like an optical illusion! (Check it out on YouTube)

They laughed and cheered. I think it reminded them of their younger days when they were strong and limber men. But I'm quite certain that none of them could do this. Not when they were young. Not when they were old. Not ever!

"Show us another one," they would demand.

So then I might fall into the Kick Worm. This is a high-energy dance that requires full body contact with the floor. Done properly—not seizure-style like the fakers flaunt—you actually look like a giant worm moving across the pavement. It's really hilarious to watch and I loved making people laugh.

Or I might break into the Smurf. This is a sexy dance with plenty of gyrating hip moves. Soul Train—the televised dance studio that taught so many of us in the 1970s and beyond the dance steps and the clothing styles of our generation—was my private instructor. (Check it out on YouTube)

By 8th grade, I was ready for the stage. So, when Dereene Middle School announced a talent show, my friend, Tony Hamilton, and I signed up. We selected the song *"Freak Out"* by Chic-Le Freak. Then summoned every locking, popping, roboting move we'd ever known and choreographed an original dance that was out of this world. We practiced the heck out of that song.

By the time the event took place—with an auditorium full of pretty girls, moms and dads, most of the school, and even our business community—we were on fire.

As soon as the director started our song, we sprung to life. As we poured out our souls—hitting every move on its mark—the audience poured out their love in shouts and cheers. This further empowered us to "become the music," which then inspired the crowd to cheer even louder. It was as if we were on an emotional trampoline, and the higher we went, the higher the crowd sent us.

When the song was over, the crowd broke out in a standing ovation. The thunderous clapping penetrated into my very bones like a jackhammer pounding on cement. I would never be the same. The audience knew we won. WE knew we had won. Everyone knew we won. And, I knew that I wanted to do this again. I liked being center stage, giving my all, to make the crowd happy.

Then the last act came on. I will never forget this student's name. Michael Speaks. He came out on stage looking like the identical twin of Michael Jackson. He had the little curl on his forehead, the jacket, the shoes, and ALL the moves. Within a few seconds of his dance, we ALL forgot about Michael Speaks. We had Michael Jackson—live and on stage—at little Dereene Middle School!

He blew the crowd away! There was no denying it. He TOOK and EARNED first place. I was so jealous of him! There was nothing anyone could have done to beat what he did. It was a one-of-a-kind perfect match—the man with the song and a mighty man at that. I had to hand it to him. Tony and I had to be content with 2nd Place.

Chapter Five

Sorting Out My Values

My mama started taking me to church when I was still in her belly. In fact, before I was conceived—when I was just a glimmer in her eye—she was toting me and all her future children into the house of the Lord.

Mama praised the Lord at church and then brought Him home—staying on her knees, begging God to help her raise eight children right and to bring her husband home safely from his long distance truck routes.

It's good she prayed too. Daddy was an exact opposite of Mama. He smoked, drank, cursed, and even smoked pot while he was driving a commercial truck. I remember one time, Mama let me ride with Dad. We traveled from Washington, D.C. and then back to our home in Savannah, Georgia.

On the way home, Dad lit a marijuana cigarette and started smoking in the truck. By the time we pulled in the driveway, I was experiencing my first and only "contact high." Mama immediately recognized that something was wrong with me and forbid me to ever ride with dad again. (Dad turned his life around when I was 23. He stopped his smoking, drinking, and drugs, and even changed his attitude about whites once he began to line his life up with Christian values.)

Nonetheless, I sorted it out. I knew Mama didn't allow Dad to smoke, drink, or use drugs in the house—sometimes he sat out in the car to do this—so I decided to keep it out of my life too.

My mother and father— Marilyn "Betty" Hamilton Byrant and Tommy Bryant, Sr.,—in 1994.

Mama and Daddy were exact opposites. Mama followed the rules, loved everyone, and stayed on her knees before God.

Daddy—son of a preacher— smoked, drank, talked bad about whites, and did his best to avoid church. After I was grown, Daddy turned his life around.

But Daddy did contribute to my moral upbringing in his own way. He used to love to go fishing with his buddy, Mr. Freeman. He'd invite me to go along, because I was the only one of his eight children that liked to fish. On these trips, Dad would give me mini-moral lessons.

For instance, Dad told me, "A man is responsible. He takes care of himself and he takes care of his own." So he never pawned his children off on his parents like some of his siblings did. He raised and paid for his own children.

He also told me, "Son, the world owes you nothing. Success comes from working hard and raising your family well."

22

Another day he added, "A man's gotta work. Getting a job is part of becoming a man." As soon as I turned 16, I followed his advice and started working. At that point, I also started contributing to the family income. If I made $100 a week, I gave Mama $30 for bills and gave Dad $20 a week for my car.

And then, of course, there was our little sex talk. Dad said something like this, "I know you are going to do it. So when you're doing it, if she gets pregnant, you better take care of your baby. You take care of your kids, you hear?" And, I listened to that too!

Mama's sex talk was similarly brief and cryptic. Of course, her first advice was for me to abstain from sex until I was properly married. Realizing that was probably not going to happen, she gave me lesson number two.

She said, "Anthony, just remember, all that glitters is not gold." What she was saying was that just because a woman looked pretty on the outside, she may not be pretty on the inside. Specifically, she may be carrying around some nasty venereal diseases. I believed Mama and took her advice to heart. I looked for a girlfriend with high values and loyalty.

Mama's cure for anxiety was simple. "While you are trying to figure it out, HE done worked it out!" Stop stressing and leave worries in God's hands.

Then Mama gave me a warning that probably caused more anxiety than ease. She assured me, "Whatever you do in the dark will eventually come out in the light." But, I think this too kept me on the straight and narrow road of morality.

Both Sides of the Bars

Mama's lesson that lodged deepest in my heart reminded me constantly, "Son, always remember, your name will take you places where money can't."

This was very inspiring for me. I worked hard to have a good name. Because of my excellent reputation, I had great opportunities—including good jobs— knocking at my door all the time.

For instance, because I could be trusted, the neighbor women who couldn't drive would ask me to run errands. They would give me a few dollars to ride my bike to Winter's store—about 3 miles away—to get them snacks. Then, I would give them back the exact change and they would give me a little pack of cookies, or some small reward.

I did this for my aunts too. My mom's sisters, Aunt Anna, Aunt Seal, Aunt Elizabeth, and Aunt Retha, would all be sitting around watching soap operas on TV. Pretty soon, they would need their fix of Pepsi sodas and pigskins. So, I'd ride my bike to pick up their party goods. On a rare good day, they would get pickled pigs feet. Now those were good. I would join in and eat along with them.

My grandparents also spoke into my life. My Grandma Evelyn Hamilton Garrett was every bit as God-fearing as Mama. She was also an encourager. One day, I told her that I was having trouble fitting in at middle school. It seemed like the boys who disrupted class were getting all the attention. I was torn. I wanted to be funny and popular. But, I also wanted to be respectful to my teacher—like I'd always been.

Grandma Garrett asked, "Would you like some Kool-Aid to drink?"

24

I said, "Sure," not realizing that she was buying a little time to pray and to think.

When she came back, she asked, "Where do *you* think you belong?"

"I want to do the right thing, but I want to have fun too. I like to make people laugh," I explained honestly.

She said, "Son, there is a time for everything. Maybe at the end of class, when the teaching is done, maybe you could make the kids laugh then. Or, maybe on the playground. Yes! That might be the best place to laugh and have fun. Get it all out on the playground."

So that is what I did! And, that's what I always loved about Grandma Garrett. She showed me how to strike a balance. She was so different from Granddaddy Bryant—my preacher grandfather.

In church or out of church, Granddaddy Peter Quincy Bryant, father of six, drew a hard line. I remember him preaching in church more than once, Deuteronomy 22:5.

In the King James Version, it says, "The woman shall not wear that which pertaineth unto a man, neither shall a man put on a woman's garment: for all that do so are abomination unto the LORD thy God."

In other words, women were not allowed to wear pants. Not even pants designed specifically for women. But didn't EVERYONE wear *robes* back in Bible times when this verse was penned? Somehow, Grandpa didn't realize that in the 1980s, EVERYONE wore pants.

Heaven forbid if a lady in pants walked into our church mid-sermon.

It didn't matter what Grandpa was preaching on—David and Goliath or the poor widow—he suddenly morphed into a "Deuteronomy 22:5 lesson."

And that word "abomination" meant that you were going to burn in Hell.

When I think back, I probably heard more of Granddaddy Bryant's words than those of just about anyone else in my life, and yet they had the least impact. That's because, unlike Grandma Garrett, his message lacked balance.

Now I did listen to his pleadings, which were based on the 10 commandments, "Don't lie, don't steal, don't cheat." That made sense to me.

But his commands, "Don't dance, don't play cards, and for girls—don't have your dress hem above the calf muscle," I didn't agree with this.

I would wade through his messages every week, because Mama took us to Grandpa's church—True Church of God in Christ Holiness Church—for a morning and evening service, virtually every Sunday. We had Sunday school from 9 o'clock to 10:30, followed by social and snack time until noon. Then, church began with songs, testimonials—with up to 20 people standing up telling what the Lord did for them this week—and finally Granddaddy's sermon.

By about 3 o'clock, Grandaddy would start singing. Sometimes he would start with a little chant. He would sing out, "God is good." Then the congregation would sing back, "All the time." Then he would change it up and say, "All the time." And the congregation would respond, "God is good."

Regardless of how he started the final part of his Sunday morning sermon, he always ended it the same way. He would sing in his big, booming voice, "It may be your last time. It may be your last time, people. It may be your last time. It may be you last time, I don't know."

Translated: You better come down and repent at the alter because if you die before next Sunday with unforgiven sins, then you will burn in Hell.

I surely did not want to burn in Hell. So I was down at the alter often, confessing to things like eating potato chips during church service, or lying to my mom when I told her I washed my hands and I didn't.

Those were my big sins because I was a squeaky-clean kid! Oh, I did commit a couple of serious sins while growing up. When I was about 13, I shoplifted. I saw a bag of Big Bol Bubble Gum in the store. I ripped open the bag and put a piece of gum in my mouth. Then, I felt so guilty that I never stole again. My conscience corrected me without anyone else having to say a word.

I guess that is one good thing that came from church. I really did believe that there was a God—which I still believe today. And, I really did believe that he sees everything that we do. I still believe that now—but there was time as a grown man when I forgot about that.

Oh, while I'm confessing, I did smoke a cigarette once. Two of my mom's brothers, Uncle Mickey and Uncle Sonny, (there were 10 kids in my mom's family) came over for a visit. Now, Uncle Mickey always kept nickels and dimes in his ashtray. I would never steal. I would ask, "Uncle Mickey, can I get the change out of your car?"

He would always say, "Go ahead," and then I would share the money with my brothers and sisters. Often there was about $2.00—which bought a lot of candy in 1979 when I was 12.

This particular time, Uncle Mickey had a cigarette that was still burning in his ashtray.

Being a curious pre-teen, I decided to take a drag. The cigarette was already burned down pretty short. Wanting to get the most out of it, I inhaled deeply.

The next thing I knew, it felt like my lungs were on fire. I was coughing and choking and couldn't catch my breath. I made such a ruckus out there in the car that it startled the adults. My mom came running out, yelling, "Anthony! Anthony! What's wrong?"

My uncles figured it out pretty quickly and they were laughing. However, Mama was not laughing. She was upset. She and God didn't believe in smoking.

Mama didn't have to lecture me. That single experiment was enough for me. I didn't like the way it felt or smelled. But mostly, I hated cigarette smoking because my dad did it so much.

As for the rest of the teenage vices—tattoos, drugs, and under-age drinking—I never did any of that. To this day, I have never experimented with drugs, I've never gotten a tattoo (which I know is safer and more popular now), and did not have my first drink until I was a married man in the United States Army.

Part of the credit goes to my five best friends. My absolute closest friend was Alphonso Thompson, who was probably raised even more strictly than I was because he was one of Jehovah's Witnesses. The other four guys were Tony Hamilton, John Lettbetter, Lewis Johnson, and Sean Quarterman.

All of us maintained very high standards—no drugs, no drinking, no smoking—because we wanted to be as healthy as possible when we competed at basketball.

Just a side note on inner city basketball—this sport transported us into another world. I repeat, basketball transported us to another world. It was what we lived for!

The basketball court was a safe place to wrestle out our identities, protect our turf, and learn the rules of life.

On the one hand, basketball was a physical sport, but it was also a battle of the minds. I was a little guy—even at age 19 only weighing 120 pounds with a 26-inch waist—playing point guard. I was the guy that brought the ball in, set up the plays, and made everyone shine. I was called upon to make split-second decisions that made the difference between winning and losing.

So when we took our Saturday trip to Lake Mayer to meet up with guys from all the different high schools—our team was usually the smallest physically. None of my group was over 5'8.

Immediately, the other teams would start with the trash talk.

"You all are nothing but boys. Go home and grow up," they taunted.

Another might add, "You boys gonna play against us? It's going to be a 'short' game. Ha! Ha! Ha!"

Their goal was to get inside our heads and beat us before we ever set foot on the court. However, we were good. We played on the court reserved for the most competitive and challenging athletes.

Our team secret was to know each other so well that we could anticipate our next moves. And my personal secret was to use my quickness and agility to steal the ball. Also, even though I didn't slam dunk—I could make a long jump shot that got the crowds attention. When that happened, it was like being on stage or being in the NBA. The feeling of group approval or group respect was out of this world.

Even though we won often—we did lose sometimes. When we were in 9th grade, we walked away from a losing game, attacking our teammates. We tossed blame around like an activated hand grenade. Someone was going to get hurt. As we matured, we learned to build one another up after our losses. We looked for positive changes we could make in our game. We also made a pact to never, never, never give up.

All in all, basketball—with my buddies including Anthony Russell—had a profound impact on my values, my identity, and my positive "team spirit" approach to life.

Just to clear up the record, it's not that I never saw any drugs or alcohol. Like I said earlier, I had these things right in my own house and definitely in our housing project. Also, I had cousins that sold drugs and were ready to "help me out" any time I wanted to partake.

But drugs just weren't for me. I saw too many teens derail their lives by using drugs. Some died emotionally. They just stopped caring and stopped living. Others died physically— in car accidents and overdoses.

I thought to myself, "I like who I am. Drugs can't make me any funnier. Drugs—including alcohol—aren't for me."

The other major contributor to my high moral standards was my neighborhood at 1900 Westlake Avenue Apartments. Now, I've already mentioned how we got along like one big family, which was 99% black. There was peace, hope, and a high level of trust in this neighborhood. But there was also FUN! Good, clean, fun.

In our neighborhood, teens didn't go clubbing to dance. We had house parties. Parents put on the music and put out the snacks and we ALL joined in the dancing. It was fun. It wasn't just the young people that liked to dance. The older ones danced too, and they could teach us a thing or two.

We didn't need alcohol or drugs to have fun. We just needed some good tunes—like the ones played on Soul Train. We tried new moves, poked fun, and had a rocking good time.

Then, at least once a year, we had a neighborhood block party. Everyone was invited. Neighborhood moms would spend hours cooking the best food, while the guys set up the giant speakers and marked out a dance floor.

Mom started letting me go when I was about 13, but she wouldn't attend because the church was against dancing. But my brother, Tommy, and I would take sodas to contribute to the event.

Before we ever left our house, the beat of the music and the smell of the food was pulling us to the party. There were BBQ ribs, fried chicken legs, hot dogs, hamburgers, chips, soda, potato salad, and sometimes even macaroni and cheese or collard greens.

Some adults had closely guarded coolers housing beer—but the whole event was so tightly supervised and so welcoming to the neighborhood children, that I never knew of a teen to cross the line.

In a word, the purpose of the block party was to create unity. In my neighborhood that took three things—eating, fellowship, and dancing!

So, I ate, talked, and danced until the moon came out. 10 o'clock was my curfew—but a boy can amass a whole lot of unity in three short hours.

A friend recently asked me, "Who paid for the block party?"

I laughed and said, "The government!"

She asked curiously, "The government?"

"Yes." I said light heartedly. "We were all on food stamps."

But I would never consider a block party a misuse of government funds. Instead, it was a wise investment in the young people. I came away from this annual event feeling that my neighbors—just like my God—cared about me, wanted the best for me, and were always, always watching me.

Chapter Six

Two High Schools

I'm not sure who was making the decisions, but when I left our predominately-black middle school, I was bused to Windsor Forest High School. Here, I was definitely a minority, but like before, everyone seemed to accept me.

This time, I made friends with Curtis Lee. Like me, Curtis was majoring in socializing and having fun. I think he and I both agreed: Why work hard to get a B when you can get a C and still pass the class?

One day, he invited me to his house during school hours to play video games. It sounded good to me. We walked a short distance across finely manicured lawns to his big beautiful house. He broke out some chips and sodas and we settled in for a marathon of video games.

He had a really cool Atari system and we spent our day playing Centipede, Pac Man, and various football, drag racing, and outer space odysseys. Gaming was so much more fun than school.

Sometimes, Curtis would invite me and sometimes he mixed and matched different teens from school. Many times, I was the only black student going into a house in this all white neighborhood—which was not common in the 1980s—but no one seemed to care.

Now, one thing that I did enjoy about my freshman year was playing on my high school basketball team. I proudly wore #35 on my shirt. However, even that was not enough incentive to stay in school.

My mom would get notices periodically that I was skipping school. She would admonish me to stay in class and I did for a spell, but then the draw of gaming would overpower me.

I thought I was doing "okay" at school until my final report arrived.

Sadly, I found out that while I passed video gaming with flying colors, I failed 9th grade. That's right. I had to repeat my freshman year.

Now you would have thought that I would have learned my lesson. But I didn't. The following year, I passed 9th grade. Then, in 10th grade I was going to fail again, but the school allowed me to take summer school.

After that, my mom had me transferred to the predominately black Alfred E. Beach High School—one of the oldest public schools in Savannah, Georgia. Mama thought that a new environment would do me good.

It wasn't that I was getting into any trouble when I was skipping school. There were no girls, drugs, alcohol, or tobacco. We were just a handful of students playing games when we should have been in school. But, who knows what all this unsupervised time could have led to over a period of time. Besides, Mama wanted me to earn my high school diploma and get on with my life.

The move did prove to be a good one. At Beach High School, I made new friends, stayed in school, and did my work. I knew many of my classmates from playing basketball at the local parks. And, even though Tommy paved the way for me at

Windsor Forest High School, I had learned the ropes of social success by the time I transferred to Beach High School.

The prior year—when I turned 16— I'd snagged my first job as a bagboy at the Food Town Grocery Store. When I arrived at Beach—I brought the total package. I had a car—a 1975 Toyota Celica Fastback –a closet full of cool clothes (and more on the way), and an unstoppable sense of humor.

Best of all, at Beach High School, I met my soulmate.

This was my 2nd Cool Car— a 1977 Nissan 300ZX — minus the cute children. They came later!

Both Sides of the Bars

Chapter Seven

In Came Red

From the first day of school at Beach High School, I received all the attention of the new kid on the block and then some. Like my mom and my grandmother, I was a positive spirit, an encourager, and downright funny.

On top of that, I had extremely good manners. I said "Yes Ma'am" and "No Sir" to every adult, at school and every place else. I opened doors for the girls, said "please" and "thank you," and was purposely considerate to all.

This, of course, got me into a little trouble. I would tell the heavy set and often ignored girls, "You look nice today." Some of these attention-starved girls would translate this to mean, "Would you be my girlfriend," and I would have to back pedal out of that notion while keeping our friendship intact.

Posing in front of our Westlake Ave apartment— dressed boldly in red.

Me—Anthony Bryant—sitting on a counter in science class at Beach High School.

Within the first week of school, I had a pack of girls flirting, flaunting, and following me around. They all wanted to see who was going to land this guy with cool clothes, a car, good manners, and a great sense of humor.

For me, it was all just fun. I wasn't really dating yet. Up until this point, I realized that I could have more fun keeping everyone on the friend level. And then I met Red. Red was in my math class.

She was everything that I wasn't. She was modest, quiet, an excellent student, and completely uninterested in me—
Anthony Bryant.

She was also extremely beautiful. She had long, black hair that was just past her shoulders. It wasn't a weave and it wasn't a wig. It was all hers and it was gorgeous. Her skin was copper toned with a sprinkling of cute little freckles that offset her bright brown eyes.

Though she was poor—and I never saw her in the latest fashion or even new clothes of the older fashion—Red made everything look good!

When I approached her, she just looked away and rolled her eyes. It was like she was saying, "Please, save your 'charm' for everyone else."

The more I tried, the harder she resisted. One day, she made it easy for me to understand. She said, "I'm not interested in being one of your groupies."

Several weeks passed and then I changed my approach. I started pursuing her when no one else was around. I noticed that Red walked home from school. She walked a couple of miles in the hot Savannah, Georgia sun. So, one day I followed her part of the way home.

Say what?

How is it that the one girl I really want—seems to be the only girl who's not interested?

When I was next to Red, I rolled down my window and said, "Hey, can I give you a ride home? It's too hot to be walking."

Barely looking at me, Red said, "I'm fine." She kept right on walking.

Not wanting to "stalk" her, I drove off.

The next day, before school dismissed, I asked her, "Can I give you a ride home from school today?"

She said, "I've got a ride. Thanks."

So, I traveled down her road and sure enough, she was walking.

I pulled up, rolled down my window, and gave her that "caught you" smile. Then, I asked, "Why did tell me you had a ride?"

She said, "I just want to walk."

Now I knew that if I could get her to smile, that I would have a chance of getting to know her. So I said with a grin, "You know, I don't bite!"

She smiled! And, she got in!

One day, at the top of the week, I asked Red if she would like to go to the movies on Saturday. *Purple Rain* was playing and it seemed like all the teens were going to see it.

Red replied nonchalantly, "I'll let you know."

Wednesday passed. No answer. Thursday passed. No answer. Friday, all through school, she didn't say a word. Finally, when I dropped her off at her house, she got out of the car, turned back, and said, "Yes, I'll go."

The next evening, when I went to pick up Red, I met her mom and her step-dad who had raised her since she was a preschooler. When they saw me—all clean cut, well-mannered, and good-humored—they welcomed me with open arms.

I was exactly the opposite of Red's last and only other boyfriend. Though an age mate, he was a genuine thug.

He messed in drugs, was involved in illegal activities, and dropped out of school. I don't know why smart and innocent girls sometimes fall for these guys, but thankfully she broke it off when things started to get ugly.

Meantime, her parents were relieved to have her dating a guy who was wholesome and clean. Her mom and I hit it off right away. She had an easy laugh and was so good-natured. Her dad welcomed me too.

Before we left, he took me outside alone and said, "Son, you are a real respectful young man and that's one thing I appreciate about you. Just don't hurt my daughter. She has been through heartbreak before with a knucklehead and I don't want her going through it again."

I said, "No sir. No sir. I will be good to Red."

At the movies, I treated her to popcorn and soda pop. She let me hold her hand for a little bit—confirming that she liked me. After the movies and a stop at Dairy Queen, we sat on her porch to talk for about 30 minutes. Then, she asked me the question that had been on her mind.

"Anthony," she asked, "am I going to be the only girl you take out or are you going to be dating other girls too?"

Red wanted commitment.

I said, "No. I don't want to take out any other girls. I only want you. Just you."

With that, we had our first kiss. It was official. Red and Anthony were boyfriend and girlfriend. I kept my word. I never dated another girl in high school, because I didn't want to.

What happened next completely surprised me. Red told me that if she was going to be my girl, then I was going to have to get serious about my future and my schoolwork.

She understood that I needed to keep my job. So, she made it easier for me by doing some of my homework. But she also taught me my classwork. It was important to her that I actually learn the material.

Many times, I'd offer to take her shopping on a Saturday. I wanted to have fun and buy something for her. She would say, "After we study. School comes first, Anthony."

Often, she would add, "Don't get all caught up in material things, Anthony. That is not what life is all about. Learn to work with what you have. And save your money. You might have an emergency."

Where does a 16-year-old girl get self-discipline and wisdom like that? Red was exactly what I needed. She transformed my thinking. Red gave me a sense of purpose. She turned my life around.

Because of Red, I changed the group of people I hung out with at school. There was no more skipping classes or goofing off. I still had fun, but I had fun with her and my basketball buddies on weekends.

At school, we were quite the couple. We were dubbed Martin and Gina from the popular black sitcom *Martin* which starred the producer, Lawrence Martin. You can check it out on YouTube, but basically, Martin was the comic and Gina was the voice of reason.

To say that Red commanded control of my life would be an understatement. I just could not get enough of her. I fell head over heels in love and everybody knew it! We even talked of marriage.

Chapter Eight

You Are Going to be a Daddy

When Red turned 16 and I turned 17, our relationship escalated. Now, in addition to going shopping or on other dates, we periodically stopped at the Budget Inn Hotel. Rooms were $26—within my budget.

For about a year, we had unprotected sex without any seeable consequences. Then, one cold, winter day, Red told me she had to talk to me. She wanted to talk *before* we went on our date.

As we sat parked in front of her parent's house, she said, "Hey, in the past few weeks I haven't had my period. It's weeks late."

She waited for that to sink in. I felt confused and panicked.

I asked, "Are you sure?"

She said, "I took a test. It came back positive. I'm going to go to the doctors to verify, but I know my body."

Then she gave voice to those shocking words, "I'm pregnant."

I said, "You're what! We've been having sex for over a year and nothing happened. How could you let this happen?"

I could see that I'd crushed her already broken spirit. Red had just told me the most upsetting news of her life—she, the A student, the voice of reason, would be spending the rest of her junior year pregnant and when she came back in the fall as a senior, she would be a mother.

She desperately needed some reassurance from me, but my mind was focused on the impact on this baby would have on my life.

My first silent thought was, "Oh my gosh! I can hear my dad now, 'What's your plan, son?'"

I told Red honestly, "I just need a few minutes to think about this."

As we sat in the car—we talked and wept. In time, I was able to assure Red that everything was going to be all right. We would work it out. I definitely wasn't leaving her or my baby. I would figure something out. Needless to say, there was no Budget Inn Hotel that night.

I didn't need to look too far for an answer. My brother, Tommy, had done the same thing a year and a half earlier. He joined the Army so he could support his new family. I decided to scrap my plans to attend the local university to get a degree in psychology. Instead, I too would join the Army.

When I told my dad that Red was pregnant, I added very quickly that I was joining the Army.

My dad sighed and said, "Okay. Now you are talking some sense, Anthony. You can take care of your child. I know you planned to go to college and your mom will be disappointed, but you can go to college later."

Telling my mom was much easier. She is an encourager and knew that now was not the time to beat me down.

After giving me a big hug, Mama said, "Anthony, I'm proud of you for doing the mature thing. You are taking responsibility for your child. You can have that baby and it will bring some focus to your life. You can do this."

I joined the U.S. Army and graduated from High School in 1986 at the age of 19. Interestingly, even though Red was helping me with math, it seemed like no one could teach me Algebra. I had to take summer school to pass Algebra before I could collect my diploma.

I am forever grateful to Mrs. Johnson. On the last day of summer school, she called me up while holding my failed final test.

As she tapped her pencil in painful indecision, she asked me, "So Anthony, what are you planning on doing after you graduate?"

"Ma'am, I'm going into the military," I said respectfully.

She glanced skyward, as if asking God himself to help her make the right decision. Then she marked my test "passed" and wished me the best!

Both Sides of the Bars

Chapter Nine

You're in the Army Now

After making the decision to enlist for three years in the Army, I enjoyed my last summer as a free man. I worked as a stock clerk at Belk department store, having worked my way up from a grocery store bag boy, to a K-Mart Super Center stock clerk, to a Kentucky Fried Chicken cook, and now this. My life was moving forward and I was feeling good about myself.

Additionally, I always saved my evenings for Red and my Saturdays for basketball with the guys. As I zipped tirelessly around the court, making long jump shots and setting my teammates up for plays, I reminded myself that I was Army ready! My body was strong and fit.

Then, my report date arrived. October 23, 1986. I reported for duty to Fort Leonard Wood, Missouri.

What I thought was going to be Basic Training ended up being Basic Torture.

"Give me 20 pushups!" the drill sergeant screamed.

"Yes, Sir!" I replied, though silently protesting. I had moved slightly while standing at attention because a bug was buzzing around my head. This nitpicking sergeant called me out for that.

Almost reading my mind, he yelled, "Listen, you scum bucket! I don't care if a bee flies up your nose and out your rear (edited version), you better not move!"

Then there was physical training. I had to do 40 military-style pushups, 62 sit-ups, and run two miles in under 13 minutes.

47

I couldn't do any of it. I was failing and it seemed as if the main goal of our drill sergeant was to break our spirit.

I can't wait until we're married Love Always E-2

I endured Basic Training—with a little "encouragement" from my dad.

Coming from Savannah, Georgia, I was not prepared for the snow and the bitter cold.

I was not the only soldier who thought about quitting.

Ultimately—I stopped focusing on the negatives and used my energy to help others meet the challenge. We were all stronger for it.

On top of all of this, we had the outings that gave Fort Leonard Wood its nickname—Fort Lost in the Woods. At 3 o'clock in the morning, we were ordered to grab our 30-pound rucksacks and head for the hills. We climbed for hours through the heavily forested Ozark Mountains.

Snow bit into our faces and it was so cold that our fingertips went numb. When we'd climbed to what seemed to be the most uninhabitable place on earth—we were ordered to set up camp. This meant we had to sleep in tiny tents on thin little mats in the freezing cold. It was horrific. Definitely, no place for a Georgia boy.

As I lay there shivering and rubbing my aching muscles, I thought about all that I'd left behind. Sunny Savannah, right on the coast of the Atlantic Ocean—so pleasant and south of the snow line. Red—my true love and best friend—always happy to see me. I just couldn't picture life without her. And, our beautiful baby girl, Tranise, born in August. I loved that little girl. Her smell, her smile—a gift into our lives from God himself.

The more I thought about it, the more I realized—my baby girl needs me. Red needs me. What am I doing running away to the Army? I need to find another way—an easier way—to care for my family.

At the next opportune time, I placed a telephone call to my dad.

"Dad," I said, "I don't want to do this. I don't want to do this."

He listened patiently as I complained about all the injustices. When I was done, he simply said, "Anthony, you're gonna do it."

Then, he hung up.

After that, Basic Training became a little easier. It wasn't just the knowledge that I had no way out. It was the fact that in the course of over 30 days, I was actually making progress. I was proving to myself that I could do what was formerly impossible.

Maybe all the verbal abuse was to make me stronger—so that I could withstand the adversity of war. I mean, what if I got captured by the enemy? They would treat me worse than this. Maybe I did need to grow thicker skin.

I decided to turn my focus away from quitting—which is an option in Basic Training—and toward encouraging others. I started helping the guys who actually told fellow soldiers that they wanted to quit.

"Don't quit," I said. "We can do this together." I reached out and helped several soldiers meet their marks in their training.

In the end, only about five soldiers out of a class of 120 quit. Thankfully, I was not one of them. I left Basic Training feeling stronger, more disciplined, and ready for life in the Army and beyond.

Age 19—US Army Basic Training was tough! I had to EARN my uniform—but boy did I look sharp! A few months later, I was at Fort Gordon Georgia for my AIT training for top-secret communications.

Both Sides of the Bars

Chapter Ten

Germany, Here I Come!

I wanted to marry Red, but just didn't see how I could support her on Army pay. Then, my commanding officer told me about BAQ—Basic Allowance for Quarters. He explained that if I was married and had a child, I would qualify for extra income. This would allow us to live off base.

Red was delighted. After completing my Advanced Individual Training (AIT)—we married. It was a small ceremony. By this time, my parents had bought their first house—4210 Worth Street—so we were married in their living room by my uncle, Elder Green Bryant. The ceremony was witnessed by my parents, Red's parents, and our beautiful 9-month-old baby girl. The date was May 5, 1987.

At the same time, my brother, Tommy, was working things out on his end to get me to Germany. Apparently, if you have a family member in the Army, you can put in a request to serve together.

Red and I married on May 5, 1987 and I brought my new little family to Germany. Oh, how I loved being a husband and a daddy. Tranise was my beautiful baby girl.

Before the year ended, my new little family was living in Germany. In fact, we were living right next door to Tommy, with his wife and daughter who was only a year and a half older than our little girl.

It was a wonderful experience. It was almost as if the Army had financed our honeymoon in a fabulous little German village in Nuremburg. Our quaint little house, coupled with immaculate cobblestone streets and friendly neighbors, made it the nicest place. Red was happy and I was happy. I couldn't wait to get home to see her and the baby every day after work. We were living like newlyweds—madly in love. We spent a lot of time with my brother's family, but we also made friends with other families. On weekends, we enjoyed sights and the German culture.

Also, we availed ourselves of German generosity. Once a year—apparently as a nation—Germans declutter. They take perfectly fine furniture and household items that they no longer need and put it in their front yard. However, instead of having a yard sale, they give it away. You haul it, you keep it!

We hauled home a handsomely carved German shrunk— which would have been way out of our budget. Basically, it is a wall unit or an entertainment center. We also spotted some nice chairs to add to our furnishing.

Germans were equally generous with their acceptance of people of all cultures. The racial tension between blacks and whites that continues to be a challenge in the US simply does not exist in this country.

As for my work, it was rewarding beyond my wildest dreams. AIT trained me to be a communications expert. After filling out the TBS/SCT 330-60e, I was awarded the highest top-secret security clearance.

Working as a Data Communications Center Operator in Nuremburg with this clearance let me receive and transmit top-secret messages all around the world.

I was hearing breaking world news before anyone else! It was fascinating work, I was good at it, and I was only 20 years old. It felt like the sky was the limit.

This picture was taken in Germany.

Life was good!

I loved my job, loved meeting so many people from around the world, and loved my little family.

Soon, our life broadened to include volunteer work. In my free time, I organized and coached the "Army Brats" basketball team. It felt good to mentor young people the way my big brother mentored me.

I remember one young man in particular, Frank. He was 14-years old when I met him. Frank was being raised by a single mom, who was called away on a mission. So, he made it his habit to take out his anger on his German Nanny and his school teachers.

I was tough on Frank. He was a great basketball player, but lousy at life skills. He needed a father-figure that he respected and even though I was only six years older than him, he responded to my discipline. More than once, I had to intercede for a frustrated teacher who was at her wits end.

I coached Frank for my entire tour of duty, but when I returned to the US in 1990, 17-year-old Frank was left behind. I always wondered what became of him. Then, the unbelievable happened.

In 1994, I took Red and Tranise to Walt Disney World in Orlando, Florida. While in town, we stopped at a grocery store. I was admiring two beautiful twin girls—still in diapers—when someone suddenly yelled, "Coach! Coach!"

I turned around and there was Frank. He was now about 6'4"—towering over me. He threw a bear hug on me and then his wife came up.

She joined our hug and said, "I feel like I already know you. I think Frank talked about you almost every day for the first year of our marriage."

Frank laughed and then added seriously, "I don't know where I would be without you, Coach. I probably would have ended up in a gang, or on drugs, or dead."

That was such a powerful and unexpected affirmation. It made me wonder how many people's lives we touch—by a few kind words or actions—having no idea of the dramatic impact.

While stationed in Germany, I also made time to play basketball with the troops. We had players—soldiers—from all across the US. These were talented guys and we played a very competitive game.

I remember well, a guy we nicknamed A.D.—initials for Basketball Hall of Famer Adrian Dantley. This guy could play ball. I'm surprised he didn't go pro. Oh my gosh, he could slam a shot, run the ball, and dominate the court. He seemed like a natural born coach too.

Then there was Chuck, a white guy over seven feet tall and very slim. I think he wore a size 16 shoe. He played center. When we chose teams, he was always picked first.

Chuck was a gentle giant—always willing to let his teammates score before he took a shot. He was just that nice of a guy. And, if anyone fouled Chuck with unnecessary roughness—both teams would gang up on the offender in defense of Chuck.

"Why'd you do that," someone would demand.

Others would chime in, "Chuck's a nice guy."

"What's wrong with you!"

"You don't do that to Chuck."

These were just two players that stood out, but there were dozens more like them. They were always ready for a hard game of basketball.

It was while I was living internationally, working with people from around the world, and playing basketball with people from all over the US—I developed a deep and enduring respect for all people. I proved to myself that Mama was right.

Both Sides of the Bars

God made all the colors, shapes, and sizes of people because he likes variety. If there was any lingering prejudice in my soul prior to joining the Army, it was all gone now.

Chapter Eleven

Numbing the Pain

Paradise was short lived. Before long, tensions in the Middle East began heating up. Every soldier—including me—was reminded that he or she could be called to the war front at a moment's notice.

In the Army, a moment's notice is literally 30 minutes. So we were required to go to bed with our rucksacks packed. As more and more soldiers began leaving for battle—I felt increasingly vulnerable. Like other family men or women, I didn't want to leave my young family behind and perhaps never return.

A few months later, so many soldiers had left the post that the University of Maryland—which had a makeshift campus on base—closed its doors. I was forced to abandon my business degree courses before ever completing a full semester.

To cope with these unsettling tremors of change, I increased my drinking. It was very gradual—so much so that Red didn't notice—but it was a real shift.

What's so amazing is that I joined the Army as a dry man—never having had a drink of alcohol. I tried my first alcoholic drink at the age of 20 in Germany, just to be sociable. My supervisor sergeant handed me a German beer – Patrizia Brau—at a barbeque.

He didn't know that I'd never had a drink before and I wasn't about to tell him. So, I accepted and attempted to take a drink like an old pro.

I took a mouthful and choked it down, but I really didn't like the taste. However, I kept working on it and finally got it all down.

Now, German beers pack a bigger punch than American beers. They simply have a higher alcohol content. So by the end of the evening—even though I'd had only one beer—I was feeling a buzz.

Over time, I developed a liking—not only for the feeling, but also for the flavor. And, wouldn't you know, of all the wonderful German beers, my favorite became Patrizia Brau. As a side note, the Germans drink their beer at room temperature, but every American soldier that I knew always iced his beers. I followed the American tradition.

As the Gulf War accelerated, television began showing footage of soldiers being beheaded or blown up. I remember an incident where a pilot was shot down and survived. The Iraqis captured him and tied him to a truck. Then they dragged him over rocks. It was slow torture and they stopped and started the agonizing process many times so that he would die slowly.

The camera never actually showed him being dragged, but as the commentator told the story, viewers saw the shredded uniform and the dry, rocky ground. Those kinds of reports really put me on pins and needles.

I kept asking myself, "When is my number going to be picked?"

The News reported the body count too. I remember hearing that the body count was up to 20. One of those dead soldiers was a really nice guy from our post. We used to play basketball together. I would give anything to remember his name. I would love to honor him. But at the time, it just made me scared.

I used alcohol to calm my nerves. Red and I always kept a few cold beers in the refrigerator to offer to guests. Initially, I only drank when we had company or if it was a big holiday. But after hearing these unsettling reports, I found myself going to the refrigerator more and more often.

Fellow soldiers serving with me in Germany.

In time, it became my daily routine to have a beer before bed to help me unwind so I could sleep. It wasn't Red and I, or anyone else sharing a beer. It was just me. I was drinking alone to numb the pain.

Then, A.D.—my basketball buddy—came back from one year in the Gulf War. Apparently, his vehicle ran over an IED (an improvised explosive device). The bomb tore up his truck and ripped up his body. He lost one arm from his elbow down, and I think three fingers on the other hand.

This was very traumatic for him and for anyone who knew him. It was like someone's worst nightmare. He left as a prime athlete, a man positive, full of promise, confident, and overflowing with energy.

He returned broken, immobilized, and maimed. Worse than his physical injuries was the assault to his spirit.

I mean, on the outside, we still knew it was A.D. But, on the inside, he appeared to be a different man. A.D. was now angry, bitter, negative, depressed and hopeless.

I tried to encourage him.

I said, "A.D., why don't you try coaching? You are really good. You know the plays and you know how to bring out the best in the other players."

He didn't seem interested. His life goal had centered around teaching his five-year-old son how to play ball even better than himself. Now, A.D. felt useless as a basketball player. In fact, he could not even shoot single-handed due to the missing fingers on his only surviving hand.

For a while, he came to the gym to watch us play. But then he stopped coming. It was likely too painful. Word spread, that like so many injured soldiers, his wife abandoned him. It seemed that he lost everything in that split-second when the bomb exploded. He lost his health, his wife, his family, and his will to live.

On the heels of that disaster, John—the cook—was called to report. Somehow, there was a breach of communication and John found out a couple of days in advance.

Now, John was one of the funniest guys that I've ever met. He was a bit overweight, and we used to tease him, saying, "The reason we don't have good food is that you eat all the good stuff and serve us the left overs."

He would laugh heartily and break into an impersonation of Chubby Checkers or a Blues Brothers routine. He was a very talented black guy and everybody loved him. He was our comic relief.

So when it came time to report—at about 3 o'clock in the morning, John was missing from roll call. They searched his room and found that he'd hung himself with a belt on the showerhead.

His roommate was crying and said, "I should have known that something was wrong. He spent the last few days giving away all of his belongings, even his favorite watch."

I felt physically sick. Being in the Army, being in Germany, being in a war wasn't fun anymore. By now, all the joy that I'd felt in the early months had completely disappeared. Daily, I was watching potential war-widows fretting and crying.

One night, I got the call. It was about 3 o'clock in the morning. That is the time that you get your 30-minute notice to report for duty when your unit is shipping out to the war front. Red and I both knew what it meant, but there was no time to linger.

Dutifully, I picked up the telephone.

"Anthony," the voice said on the other end of the line.

"Mama," I said, both shocked and relieved.

She could never get the time zones right and so on more than one occasion, she about gave me a heart attack when she called in the wee hours of the morning.

Then, I heard that Chuck was coming home—missing one leg. Somehow, they'd alerted his wife and she told some other Army wives. Before long, the news became widely known. For about three weeks, we dreaded the day that our star center would return to our base.

As days passed, it broke my heart to know the enemy had broken his body. Had it broken his spirit too? The only thing I had to go by was how A.D. had changed completely after his injuries.

One day, we were in the gym in the middle of an intense game when we heard a familiar voice call out, "I've got next."

It was Chuck. His comment, coming from his wheelchair, was meant to be a joke. He broke the ice just like he intended to and we all gathered around our friend.

Getting a better look, he really did lose a leg. He lost it all the way up to his pelvis. But he did not lose his spirit. We got the whole Chuck back.

He had his same heart, his same positive energy, and his same gentle spirit.

Chuck told us, "I may use my loss as a type of platform to help disabled veterans who are going through this same challenge. I want to help other people—other families—heal and get on with their lives."

Chuck's wife stayed by his side. Before long, his prosthetics arrived and he was back on the court. He could never run as fast or guard as well, but Chuck could still make his shots. We were happy to have him play with us—he still got picked. One of the greatest assets that he offered the team was a sense of humor, a sense of perspective, and a sense of brotherhood.

Still, at the end of the day, I knew that Chuck only had one leg. I loved my sports. I loved my body. I loved my family. I didn't want to lose an arm, or a leg, or my life.

By the time my tour ended in Germany, it took a lot more than a beer or two to numb my pain. I graduated to Seagram's gin and Crown Royal.

Both Sides of the Bars

Chapter Twelve

Three More Years

I still had a family to support—so I decided to enlist for three more years. After all, trying to line up a job in the US from Germany was impossible for a guy like me. I'm not an on-line or mail order job applicant. One way or another, I'm going to facilitate a personal interview.

While the Army makes no guarantees, I was told that there was a good chance that I could pull my next three years at Hunter Army Airfield in our hometown of Savannah, Georgia. That is exactly what happened.

Red was glad to be home. As you can imagine, both sets of grandparents were delighted to indulge four-year-old Tranise. And I had a chance to reconnect with my friends from school and the basketball court. Some of my classmates now worked at local stores, one was a fire fighter, a few went to college, and one was a police officer like my brother, Tommy.

We were all growing—Red, Tranise, and me.

It was good to be stateside again to meet up with family, friends, and classmates.

As for me, I kept my job. The only thing that changed is that I was now receiving and transmitting top-secret information around the world from Savannah. It was still fascinating and I even considered extending my enlistment. That is, until the Army wanted to send me to Korea for a year.

Korea is one of the few deployments where the Army will not pay for you to bring your wife and children. I'm not sure if it's due to the high risk of the assignment or if it's because your tour will only last for 12 months.

Either way, Red and I didn't want to be separated for 12 months. We had a good thing going. As a matter of fact, Red was my first real girlfriend—I'd never had sex with anyone else—and I wanted to keep it that way.

So as my discharge date neared, I began to apply for jobs on my days off. Initially, I wanted to stay in communications. With my security clearance, there were many high paying jobs in the government and in the private sector. On the other hand, my brother, Tommy, was encouraging me to continue to follow in his footsteps.

I'd followed him into the military and that worked out well. Now, I had a chance to follow him into law enforcement. One thing I knew for sure—I liked the uniform.

Then, one night I saw a car pulled over by the police. As I took a closer look, I saw that the officer was none other than my big brother, Tommy. The lights on his police car were flashing and the whole scene looked so cool.

I decided to take his advice. However, when I was in a position to apply, the Savannah "City" Police Department was no longer hiring. So, I put in my application with the Chatham

County Sheriff's Department. With my outstanding military record, I was hired quickly. And actually, a very high percentage of law enforcement officers are former military personnel, because they use the same command model.

In May of 1992, I received an honorable discharge from the military.

Both Sides of the Bars

Chapter Thirteen

Qualifying to be a Corrections Officer

I don't want to make it sound as if a military background is a shoo-in for law enforcement work. The interview and admission process is extremely rigorous. In a nutshell, law enforcement seeks to hire people who are *healthy*. That means mentally (thinking ability), physically (body fitness), emotionally (coping skills and self-management), and spiritually (sound moral values).

Some indications of " good health" are how well connected you are to your family, friends, community, church or club, hobbies, neighbors, fitness program, and core values.

Most importantly though—applicants must be honest. For instance, on the written and oral test, applicants are asked if they've ever stolen anything. That might be question 50. Then, question 87 might ask applicants: "How did you feel when you stole a pencil from work?" By asking similar questions in slightly different ways, the department does its best to figure out the real character and fitness of each applicant.

I passed the entrance exams along with the physical fitness test with flying colors. I genuinely loved people, liked to follow the rules, and was extremely well connected and balanced.

Then, came the scenarios. As an applicant to be a jailer at the Chatham County Detention Center—a holding center for suspects awaiting sentencing—the department needed to answer another question. Where do my loyalties lie?

To discern this, a half-dozen high-ranking officers presented real life situations and rated my responses. Of these, the following is the most challenging for most applicants.

Scenario: *You—a corrections officer— are walking through the cell block when suddenly the trustee (an inmate with work privileges) grabs your partner. He puts a shank (homemade knife) up to your partner's throat and yells, "Give me your keys or I will kill your partner?"*

What will you do? Put your hand over the rest of this page and think about this. What will you do if your partner's life is on the line? Do you protect your partner or protect your keys?

If you are like most people, you will save your partner's life. Then, you and your partner and backup help will deal with the errant inmate and the missing keys.

WRONG!

A corrections officer never ever gives up his keys. Think about it. Why does the inmate want the keys? Once he has the keys, he can order you to back up. Then, he can unlock one cell and give the keys to the newly released inmate who can then unlock all the other cells. Now, you have the inmates running the prison, which is dangerous for everyone.

You may protest—but what if he kills my partner? The truth is: When an inmate gets to that level of defiance, he doesn't care anymore. He's likely to kill your partner, no matter what you do.

Here is how I answered. *"I would tell the trustee, 'I will not give up my keys under any circumstances. It's up to you* what you decide to do with my partner. The law will contend with you later. But you are not getting my keys."

When asked to explain my position I said, "If I give him my keys, the chances are, he's going to open the floodgates for all the other inmates. And he's probably going to kill my partner anyways. So I will never give up my keys."

Big grins spread across all their faces. That question was the deal breaker for so many applicants and once again, I'd passed. Now in the spirit of being 100% honest in this book, I will tell you—someone coached me on this. Had I not been told the "correct" answer and the reason for it—I too would have erred on the side of compassion for my fellow officer.

I traded in my military uniform for a Chatham County Sheriff Corrections Officer uniform.

Though I was aiming to be a police officer—this proved to be an excellent stepping stone.

As always, I treated everyone with respect and dignity.

Chapter Fourteen

Psychological Warfare

Long-term inmates are master influencers—master manipulators. Their world has shrunk drastically. They have lost the right to differentiate themselves by anything money can buy—nice houses, fancy clothes, fast cars, and influential friends. The only currency left is information.

Because of this, corrections officers get extensive training on how to protect themselves from seemingly "innocent" yet carefully concocted schemes and scams—all based on information.

The Slickster

The slickster appeals to the corrections officer's emotions. Inmates listen for tiny threads of information that can be weaved into a coat of deception custom fit for each officer.

In one case, a female officer was having problems with her boyfriend. While on duty, she accepted a cell phone call and vented her frustrations.

A slickster overheard the conversation and started a subtle dialogue with the officer. As she walked by, he gently smiled and said, "You look really nice today."

That was it. That was his first move. She was a heavyset girl, feeling undervalued, and suddenly she was getting some much needed attention from a hunk of a man. These men are built—they work out all day—and they have nothing better to do than to figure out how to worm their way into a lonely heart.

A few days later, he noticed her new haircut. In a few sentences, he revealed that he not only remembered her old cut,

75

but had an observation as to "why" this new style was such a good match for her. Now he had two threads.

A few days later, she changed the color of her nails. He made a joke—asking if she could get some nail polish for him so they could match—and she started laughing.

From there, it was quick work to wrap her up and reel her in. The next thing she knew, they were touching hands, kissing, and then having sexual relations. In doing this, the officer broke her employment contract and lost her job. The inmate broke her heart but not his—because to him it was all a game.

Lesson: 1) Corrections officers are advised to leave cell phones in the car. If there is a true emergency, calls can be made to the office of the prison. 2) Picture invisible ears everywhere—on the walls, on the floors, on the ceiling, and in the air—and refuse to share any personal information at work.

The Gambler

Inmates have very little control over their own lives. So they find great pleasure in controlling other people's lives. One of the easiest ways to do this is to gamble.

An inmate who is new to the center may be looking to fit in or be entertained. He may accept a seat in a card game to gamble for something as little as an item on his meal tray. If all goes according to Hoyle—the other inmates will let him win a little bit. The greenhorn is unaware that the other inmates at the table are working as a team against him.

About the time the new guy gets confident and makes a bigger bet—they shut him down. Now—he owes them. In prison, if you owe me—I OWN you. You become my servant. I may use you to run in-house errands or to be my "woman" or anything in between.

Lesson: Corrections officers are the only ones authorized to run the prison. It is the officers job to supervise well enough so that the rule of "no gambling" is enforced. This protects everyone.

The Silent One

Some inmates isolate themselves. They don't want to attach themselves to anyone. They just want to die—literally. Sometimes, it is because their crime has ripped such a rupture in their lives that they don't think they can ever recover. Or, the pain and shame of their conviction is just too heavy to bear.

For others, they come into the prison environment so ill-equipped, that they become easy pickings for the manipulators and dominators. Aggressive inmates can smell fear like frying bacon—the scent is undeniable! They will use threats and force to get what they want and then pass the victim around like a volleyball to other inmates.

Once the victim is convinced that this is never going to change—his all-consuming thought is to plan his suicide.

Lesson: It is the corrections officer's job to keep everyone safe. That includes the responsibility to proactively give options to the "silent ones." Such options include counseling, transfer to another cell block, or checking oneself into isolation (away from all other inmates).

The Confidant

This inmate is usually a likeable guy. He'll say, "I'm your man. If you want to know anything about contraband (items not allowed for inmates) or anything going on, I'm your guy."

His goal is to gain your trust—one secret at a time—until you begin to trust him more than you trust your fellow officers. When that happens—you are now his flunky! You are walking to the beat of his drum. He is pulling your strings.

Left unchecked, he will begin to cause a division between you and your fellow officers. He will say things like, "I know Officer Smith is a nice guy, but I heard him say this about you."

These little wedges can destroy an officer's team. For inmates, pulling the strings on their superiors is a whole lot more fun than watching television.

Lesson: Corrections officers need inmates to give them valuable information. The issue here is not information. It is trust and subtle manipulation. Officers must constantly monitor their own feelings of loyalty and stay true to the brotherhood of officers.

One way to do this is to periodically ask yourself: What is this inmate's agenda? Then ask: What is my agenda? The answer to the second question needs to be: I'm a team player with my officers to supervise, ensure safety, engage, enforce, and encourage all inmates.

The Buddy

Now here is an inmate that is offering you nothing but friendship. And there are some really cool people in prison. There are good people that made a bad decision. They will pay their time, get released, and go back to their *original* values.

However, there are also thugs and manipulators who use honey sweet goodness to attract conversations and then sting you the first chance they get.

This happened to me. One day an inmate said, "Merry Christmas."

I liked this guy. I smiled and hollered back, "Merry Christmas to you."

Then he said, "Have you gotten all your shopping done?"

I said, "No, I've got two more gifts to get."

He sid, "Oh. Oh. You probably live 30 minutes from the store. You're going to have a hard time getting two gifts and getting home on time."

Without thinking, I said, "No. I only live 10 minutes from here and then it's only another 15 minutes to the mall."

A few weeks later, in the midst of a casual conversation, he said, "I bet you live in a little brick ranch with a white picket fence."

I smirked and said, "You got the wrong guy." I then went on to describe my apartment on the Southside in fairly general terms, but still giving him clues.

After a few months, of seemingly playful banter, he knew exactly where I lived. Then came the threat. I insisted that he follow a rule and he insisted on an exception.

When that didn't work, he threatened, "Listen. I know exactly where you live, Cambridge Square Town Homes. My people watch your little girl and baby boy playing outside in the yard all the time."

"What!" I said in shocked disbelief. His words ripped my world wide open. Now I was afraid for the safety of my family.

A few weeks later, I was out washing my car and I saw a suspicious vehicle driving up and down my road in front of my house.

Thankfully, nothing ever happened. But it was a real wake-up call.

Lesson: Trust no one on the other side of the bars.

Chapter Fifteen

Let's Get Physical

One thing that appealed to me about work as a corrections officer was that I would be helping people who needed a hand up. These were my people. I was back in Savannah, Georgia—my hometown—and this was a chance to give back.

I knew *why* some of these men were in here. They felt hopeless. They were raised in poverty and neglect, abused in their own homes, and never shown a better way.

I figured that as a "hometown boy" and a corrections officer, I could reach out to the underdogs and encourage them to build a better future by earning their GED, enrolling in Life Skills classes, and making a plan for when they were released.

In the meantime—while paying their debt in prison—I could ease their stay by listening to their stories and lightening things up with my sense of humor. I could believe in them.

Then came the physical training. I found out that I would be going into the prison—with up to 20 inmates loose at one time—armed with only my name badge, my radio, and my keys.

Now this might not be a problem for some guys. Some men like to brawl and fight. But that's not me. I was real clear on the fact that inmates can be angry, violent, and unpredictable.

I paid close attention as we were taught self-defense tactics, but frankly, that stuff just didn't seem to work for me.

For a moment, I began to reconsider. Maybe there was a better way to help the underdogs than by working in the prison. After all, I'm a small guy.

At the time—in 1992—I was military tough, but still only 5'7" and 135 pounds. And remember, all my military duty was non-combat.

But in the end, I decided to go through with it. For one reason, I was already committed and I needed this job. My wife was pregnant with our second child—Anthony Bryant, Jr.—and that weighed heavy on my mind. And, I reminded myself that this was a quick stepping stone to becoming a fully armed police officer.

My son—Anthony Bryant, Jr.—was born when I was serving as a Chatham County Corrections Officer in Savannah, Georgia.

I was so proud of him!

Corrections officers training also taught me to run toward a prison riot—something counterintuitive for sure. But our focus was to save our fellow officer —who'd sounded the alarm for back up.

So just a little back story: Everyone who works at a prison (at least Chatham County Detention Center) is trained to back up the corrections officers on duty if they sound the alarm. So civilians supervising in the kitchen, or maintenance workers, or office staff—they are all trained to rush to the support of an officer in need.

Now they didn't come in unarmed. In this situation—when the alarm is sounded—we all put on riot gear. This full body armor—along with a billy club and sometimes mace—helped us subdue the riot very quickly in most cases.

In fact, once we started rushing into "combat"—most of the inmates would either go to their cells or surrender by lying down on the floor. Those who chose to fight would lose privileges—anything from isolation to losing visitation.

Training also included the mandate for corrections officers to wait for back up before engaging in physical contact. In the case of a riot, the corrections officer assigned to the rioting unit could lock himself in the "hub" behind metal doors until back up arrived.

We also used riot gear when an inmate refused to come out of a cell. There might be 10 inmates in the cell, but the court only requested one. If he was unwilling to come out with his own free will, we had to put on riot gear and go in as a team to extract him.

In most instances, that solved the problem, because if any inmates fought on his side, they lost privileges too. Most inmates were not willing to lose even more rights for another inmate—especially when they knew that they couldn't win.

When I multiplied the psychological and the physical demands of the job, it equaled high stress work. I took it on, but I also increased my drinking –my liquid courage—to face the challenge.

Chapter Sixteen

Working with Dynamite

Inmates can be like ticking time bombs. No one knows for sure what is going to set off an inmate—but he can explode like dynamite with the slightest friction.

By means of a phone call, a personal visit, or even through the grapevine, an inmate may learn of news that would make any man angry. But in prison, he is powerless to act.

For instance, an inmate may find out that his wife is divorcing him, his daughter was molested by a longtime "friend" of the family, his mom died and he can't attend the funeral, his son joined a gang, or his court appeal was denied.

Each of these events leads to pain and pain usually manifests itself in anger. That anger has to go someplace and it is usually directed at fellow inmates or the corrections officer.

When I heard about these things or noticed that someone's disposition had changed—I would try to reach out and do what I could to comfort him.

Sometimes I would allow the hurting inmate some extra privileges. I might allow him to take a shower to cool down. Or, to work out a few extra minutes after everyone else returned to their cells. In my book, my job was to be firm but fair.

Other corrections officers were more by the book. The rule is: No talking after midnight. But a hurting inmate might have found a listening ear at 12:30. By active listening, the fellow inmate could encourage the victim to *quietly* convert his pain into words and thereby let it out amicably.

However, a hardnosed corrections officer might demand, "I said shut it up or I'll write you up."

One such corrections officer did just that, even though the other cell mates were not complaining. The next day, the angry inmate threw feces on him.

On the other hand, if the inmates believe that you respect them and have their best interests at heart, they will protect you.

I remember one time a new inmate came into my section. He had a chip on his shoulder from a previous prison experience. He had the mentality that it was him against the officers and all officers were evil.

He started yelling at me and cursing me before I even had a chance to say hello. But before he said too much, two strong inmates stepped up and said, "Hey man. That's Mr. Bryant. He's okay. He's cool."

When the new inmate cooled down, they added roughly, "Don't you ever be talking to Mr. Bryant like that again."

Chapter Seventeen

Bloopers

Even with the best training, there are some things you have to figure out for yourself. One of the first scams the inmates got over on me involved the food trays.

At Chatham County Detention Center, we didn't have the old fashioned "Andy Griffith" cell bars. We had solid metal doors that afforded complete privacy. There was a slit in the door with a lid that could be lifted so that officers could peek in. This opening also served as the door to pass in the food trays.

On my first day, I passed the trays in—one after another—with no problem. Then, I suddenly heard a crash. Clearly, the tray had landed on the floor.

I said, "I'm sorry. That was my fault. I must have pushed it in too far. I'll get you another tray."

That went on, in various cells, for several days. Then one day, the trustee (an inmate trusted to mop the floor) pulled me aside and clued me in.

He said, "They're scamming you, Mr. Bryant. They are dropping an empty tray on the floor so that they can get TWO trays."

I wised up, thanked the trustee, and gave HIM two trays that night for the tip.

Inmates would do the same type of scam with their pillows. Prison pillows are only about an inch thick. You could easily fit four prison pillows into a standard pillow case.

One inmate came up and said, "Mr. Bryant, someone stole my pillow."

"Are you sure?" I asked.

"Yes, come look."

Sure enough, there was no pillow. So I gave him another pillow. Later, I found that some inmates had three or four pillows stuffed in their cases. It was an age-old scam.

My last blooper was really too big to be termed an embarrassing error. It was probably a warning sign that I wasn't processing my job stress in a healthy way. On the home front, life was good. Tranise—soon to be seven—loved her three-month-old baby brother, and Red loved us all.

It was about eight months into my job—almost through my probation—when I showed up for work drunk. The rule was—automatic firing! You cannot break this rule while on probation. Period.

However, instead of firing me, the supervisors sent me home for three days without pay and started my probation over. To my knowledge, this had never been done before.

My superiors made an exception because they really liked me. I worked well with the inmates. I genuinely respected the prisoners and they responded to my encouragement. Additionally, everyone—on both sides of the bars—liked my lighthearted humor.

When I returned to work, I thought this had all blown over. Then, when I was making my rounds one of the inmates became a "confidant."

"Mr. Bryant," he said softly, while motioning me to come over.

He continued, "I know the other officers are good people, but I heard them talking about you."

"What did you hear?" I asked.

He looked me squarely in the eyes—so as to meter my reaction—and then said, "They said you came into work intoxicated and were suspended for three days. They weren't too happy about that."

Instantly, I felt hurt and angry. These officers knew better than to let sensitive personal information leak out into the prison population.

"What did they tell you?" I demanded.

He said, "Oh. They didn't tell me anything. They were telling each other and I just overheard. But I thought you would want to know. I like you, Mr. Bryant."

Still not sure that he was telling me the truth, I asked, "What are the names of the officers that you heard talking?"

He listed off three names, two males and a female.

The names added up.

He said in a caring voice, "You tell me if I ain't right."

I pushed my surging anger aside long enough to part cordially, saying, "Thank you, Mr._____."

Then, I talked to the disgruntled officers.

I said, "Mr. _____ said that he overheard you talking about me getting suspended. What is going on? We have got to be tighter than that!"

Officer A said, "We didn't know he overheard. You know that we would never do that on purpose. But frankly, we don't think that it's fair that you got slapped on the wrist for coming in drunk while you're on probation."

Officer B chimed in, "Yeah. Why are you getting special treatment? I've been working here for five years—doing my job and got written up for being late one time last week. How's that fair?"

Officer C said, "Why would you come in drunk anyways? You know you put everyone at risk when you do something like that."

I said, "I'm sorry. I never ever should have come in drunk and I promise that I'll never do that again. But we have to solve this thing because we need to be able to count on each other when we need back up. We can't have any unresolved junk between us."

I continued, "I know that I started this whole mess. I accept total responsibility for my actions and I'm asking you to forgive me and put this behind us. Can you do that?"

Officer B said, "This is just further proof that the system is unfair. I don't like it when people get preferential treatment."

"Listen," I said humbly, "I can't control what the supervisors do. You are right. I deserved to be fired. But I can promise you this, I'll do my very best to support all of you from now on and that means never letting that incident happen again. Can we work together?"

Officer A said, "He's right. Anthony didn't make the call on his suspension. And we did wrong too. We never should have been talking behind his back—especially in ear shot of the inmates. So, I will accept your apology and I'm sorry for what I did."

"What about you two?" I asked. "For the sake of professionalism and the safety of us all, can we put this behind us and move forward?"

Reluctantly, they agreed. Our relationship was never 100% mended, but we did move forward. I felt that if I needed back up, they would be there in an instant.

In the meantime, Mr. Confidant asked me if his information was useful. I acknowledged that it was and that the issue was resolved. He agreed to keep quiet about the issue and then said, "You know, I feel extra hungry tonight."

I took the hint and gave him an extra food tray.

On another day, he wanted an extra 15 minutes of recreation time after the others left the area. I allowed it. These were small allowances that I could make.

Then, he asked me for a cigarette. Now that is breaking policy, so I said, "No."

It's not surprising that he asked. He was testing me to see just how far I would go. He found out. I would not break policy to repay a favor.

Actually, just for a point of interest, most prisons outlawed cigarettes and fried food years ago. Prisons have to bear the healthcare costs of the prisoners, they will not allow products or foods that have been proven to cause cancer or disease.

Both Sides of the Bars

Chapter Eighteen

The Daily Routine

Working as a corrections officer was actually like having three jobs. For two weeks, I worked first shift, from 8 o'clock in the morning until 4 o'clock in the afternoon. Being a morning person, this was my favorite job.

"Hey man, how's it going?" I'd ask with a smile.

"Going good with me," an inmate would banter. "But you must be feeling really bad after your team got whipped last night."

"They'll be back," I replied. "It's part of their long-term strategy. They are just letting your team *think* they can win. We'll get you in the play offs," I added.

These inmates—the first shift crew—were generally in a pretty good mood. It was a new day, breakfast was on the way, and visitors would soon be pouring in. These visitors might include outside people who teach GED classes or Life Skills classes, or counselors, or chaplains who make day visits.

For the most part, busy inmates are happy inmates. Also, this was a very structured part of the day. The routine included recreation time and two of the three meals served.

So I spent most of my time engaging the inmates. I tried to encourage the ones who were trying to improve their lives and inspire the ones who were not. All of it was done in a spirit of genuine respect and concern.

Plus, I knew some of these guys. Every once in a while, a guy that I played basketball with would be admitted.

"Anthony," he'd say, almost relieved to see a friendly face.

"Hey, man. Sorry you're in here," I'd reply. "How are you doing?"

No matter who they were, though, I didn't give special favors. If they were in, they were in to do their time and I'd treat them fairly. If it ended up that someone gave me some needed information or helped me out, I would be fair and give that inmate a minor reward such as an extra tray or an extra shower. But that was it. No favors.

In being so open and caring, I met a lot of quality men. Sometimes, after weeks of positive conversation with an older man, I would ask, "What are you doing in here? You don't belong in a place like this. Why are you here?"

One older man told me, "I just made a mistake."

Another said, "Ain't always been like this. I was a really bad person years ago and I just let it continue on. But I'm too old for that now. I had to change my ways."

It was men like this who I appointed as trustees. Trustees could be trusted to mop the floors or clean the restrooms or do other paid work while the other inmates were in their cells.

Second Shift

When two weeks were up on the first shift, I rotated to the second shift. This was my second favorite job. The crew of inmates was now changed. Same bodies but different attitudes. This shift ran from 4 o'clock in the afternoon until midnight.

This shift is similar to police work. Not too much crime happens during the workday. But from 4 o'clock to midnight— crime rises. In the civilian world, this is because people come home from work tired. Domestic violence goes up—people can't fight when they are at their separate jobs. Drinking and drug abuse escalates and all that this entrails. And people are overall more restless when they are less structured.

During this shift, inmates spent 99% of their time in the common day room. They talked, watched television, played cards, and hung out. As the evening wore on, it got harder to pass the time and tensions could escalate. It was my job to watch, to notice, and to keep everyone safe.

I remember early on in my career. I was sitting safely at my desk—which was surrounded by a yellow square of tape on the floor, creating about a 5-foot safety zone for me. If an inmate had a problem—we need more toilet paper in the bathroom—he could approach my desk.

However, he couldn't cross the yellow line without being invited. If he did, he would lose some of the few privileges that he had. This included loss of commissary privileges (couldn't buy snacks or personal items), loss of telephone privileges, or loss of visitation.

This may not seem like much, but when your world is already too small for comfort, losing one of these privileges can make it almost unbearable.

So on this particular day, I was sitting comfortably in my taped in safety zone when suddenly I heard, "Bang!" I looked up and someone had flipped over a table. Three black guys jumped a white guy.

Immediately I used my radio to call for backup. Within minutes, back up was there and we broke up the fight.

As I talked to each of the inmates involved, it became apparent that they'd been gambling. It was a set up. The three blacks teamed up against the white inmate and then accused him of cheating. A fight broke out.

They were all written up, because they were all breaking the rules. All of them knew that gambling was not allowed. But I had to accept part of the blame.

Had I been walking around—in the group—doing a better job supervising and engaging, I probably could have prevented this. In fact, that is what I did. From that point forward, I did a better job of staying involved.

Part of my job on this shift included shakedowns. Every so often—unannounced to the inmates—I would go into their cells and look for contraband. Contraband was any item smuggled into the prison. It could include shoes, clothes, ink pens, or anything else that was not issued from the facility or bought in the commissary. But mostly, it was cell phones, drugs, or alcohol.

These items were usually brought in by corrections officers who'd gotten tangled in the web of "the slickster." While I was working at the Chatham County Detention Center, one of the officers fell victim to this.

I heard that it happened this way. During visitation, an inmate received a visit from his girlfriend. She brought one of her girlfriends with her. They were knockout gorgeous, Hispanic girls.

When the visit was over, the corrections officer asked, "Who was that girl?"

The inmate boasted proudly, "That was my girlfriend."

The officer asked, "Who was the other girl?"

The inmate said, "That was her friend."

The officer smiled and said, "She's beautiful!"

Now for the officer, it all ended there. He'd seen an unusually beautiful woman, made a comment, and that was that. However, for the inmate, the wheels began to turn. He saw a commodity that he could trade with. In short order, the inmate and his girlfriend were scheming for a way to get the officer in their pocket.

A few days later, the inmate said to the officer, "Are you married?"

"Why would you ask that?" he said.

"That girl who was in here with my girlfriend, she thinks you're cute. She asked my girlfriend if you're married," the slickster said.

Now, the officer's ego was getting involved. A beautiful girl was interested in him. Maybe it was the uniform! Maybe it was his power. Or, maybe she thought his chubby little face really was cute. It doesn't matter. He wanted to see her.

Soon, dates were set up. Each time the officer and the beauty went out, the officer brought something in for the inmate. Eventually, the contraband was discovered and traced back to this errant officer. He lost the girl—mere bait—and his job. The inmate lost a few privileges.

Oh, and once on second shift I was called in to break up a riot. When I got the call, I sent all the inmates for lock down. Then, I jumped into my riot gear and about 100 of us stormed into the cell block.

The officer on duty had secured himself in the hub. When he let us in, we were confronted by dozens of inmates with towels around their heads. This was there defense from the mace we were about to unload.

When they saw us storm in—combat ready—most of them fell on the floor in surrender. Others ran off to their cells. I only had one encounter. On my way across the room, a guy who was already down kicked me in the shin. My body armor did it's job and I barely ended up with a red mark on my body.

In fact, in my three years of service as a corrections officer, that was my worst injury sustained.

However, I don't want to make it sound like this was an easy job. Being a corrections officer on the first two shifts was somewhat like being a nanny. My job was to keep everyone safe and cared for. But it was like being a nanny for a pack of pit bulls. For the most part, the pack did as it was told. But at any moment, emotions could escalate and violence could break out.

It was this feeling of vulnerability—one unarmed officer surrounded by 20 inmates—that keep me in a state of tension.

I knew that if they wanted to, these inmates could kill me in 10 seconds. Sure, I might have had time to radio for back up. But by the time they arrived, I'd still be dead. So my mind was on high alert. This hypervigilant tension kept me alive, because I was able to detect the smallest sign of anger and defuse it before it got dangerous.

Second shift was particularly difficult to unwind from because when I arrived home, Red was already sleeping. She didn't want to hear about the trials or antics of my day because she had to be rested for her job in the morning. Also, she'd worked all day and then wrestled with the needs of the children. So this was a tough two-week shift.

Third Shift

Third shift—midnight to 8 a.m.—could be summed up in one word. Boring. Everyone was in lockdown for the night. There was no one to talk to and nothing to do. The hardest part of the job was finding a way to stay awake.

The corrections officer still had to walk through the facility periodically to make sure everyone was safe. When I did my first few walk throughs early in the shift, I tried to make myself known.

I whistled, sang a song, walked with heavy steps. This is to alert the inmates that I'm coming. Among other things, homosexual relations was against the rules. I didn't want to catch these guys and write them up—so I tried to be fair.

As a matter of fact, I was beyond fair. If I caught a couple of guys for the first or second time, I'd say, "Stop doing that!" and give them another chance.

But everyone has their limits. If I went to all the trouble to let you know that I was coming, and then I peeped in the door flap and caught you in the act—then I would say, "You *want* to be written up."

For this rule breaking, it was usually a month without commissary, phone, or visits. It was one of those three punishments.

As you would expect, there are corrections officers that take the opposite approach. They actually tiptoe down the hall and try to catch inmates in the act. This, to me, is not a good strategy for building trust and a spirit of fairness. In the end, a corrections officer of this sort is much less likely to get the protection of the inmates if trouble breaks out. In fact, he is probably making himself a target.

While consensual sex is against the rules, rape is not tolerated. It's not that it doesn't happen, but it carries much heavier consequences. The rapist will end up being sent to the hole—isolation for 30 days—and is never put in the same dorm with the victim again. That usually cures the problem.

Now, whereas the corrections officer cannot prevent a rape, the victim can. I've seen guys buy some time when threatened with rape.

One guy said to his potential rapist, "Let me just get my dinner in me and then we'll do it."

Then, when he saw the corrections officer at dinner time, he told him of the threats. The officer removed him from the cell.

Another guy, when I was walking the hall, opened his door flap and yelled, "Get me out. Get me out. He's going to kill me. He's going to choke me out."

When an inmate yells for help, I have to take action. It's now part of public record and everyone knows that he pleaded for help. If I don't get him out and keep him safe, the Center can be sued.

I know of one case where an open homosexual pleaded to come out because he was being threatened with rape. The hardened corrections officer left him in, figuring, "You're a homosexual. You get what you deserve."

Ultimately, the corrections officer got what he deserved. He deserved to be fired, because no body—homosexual or straight—deserves to be raped.

In the Chatham County Detention Center, I would be surprised if over 10% of the inmates were raped. It's not nearly as bad as it is in high security prisons. But it still happens.

If an inmate is threatened or believes that he is targeted to be a victim—he can request isolation. He will be in solitary confinement for 23 hours a day—with books and cards—and let out 1 hour a day for a shower and solo recreation. This is a really tough way to protect yourself.

Most of the rapes that I became aware of happened to young men—timid, scared, and completely uneducated about prison life. When they came into the facility, a slickster would offer them food and friendship. The next thing the kid knew— he "owed" this guy something. That something was sex. Either he gave "willingly" or the slickster told him, "If you try to run or tell on me, I've got five guys to finish the job."

It's sad, but no one sits an inmate down and tells him the rules. The system is designed in such a way that it sends the message: You messed up. You figure it out. You figure out how to survive in prison.

Both Sides of the Bars

Chapter Nineteen

Basic Law Enforcement Academy

My intention was to help inmates change their lives. However, it only took a few months for me to realize that they—for the most part—didn't want to make a change. Way too many prisoners used the Chatham County Detention Center as their personal hotel, sometimes checking back in on the very day they were released.

The more I thought about it, the more I realized that I was serving time right along with them. Eight hours a day, I was confined to a correctional facility with pretty much the same restrictions that they had. There were only a few important differences: I was accountable for everyone's safety and I got to go home every night. I really felt like my life had stalled.

So at the first opportunity, I enrolled in the Basic Law Enforcement Academy. As I learned the new skills required to pursue in a high speed chase, or to control a subject while making a proper arrest, or even something as simple as directing traffic when a stop light blew out—it made me realize how I could perform a "real" service to my community.

I wanted to serve and protect the people who were contributing to my hometown of Savannah, Georgia. I wanted to make the streets safe for my neighbors who were driving to work, paying taxes, and supporting the schools, the parks, and yes…even the prisons.

I wanted to be a role model, someone that young people—or anyone—could look up to.

On October 24, 1993, I graduated and was promoted to Deputy Sheriff. Immediately, I applied to both the city and the county to be a police officer. Neither were hiring at the time. So, I waited. And waited. And waited.

I kept in touch with people who were already working as police officers.

"Tommy," I asked my brother, "when is the City going to be hiring?"

"I don't know, man," he replied. "Soon, I hope. You're going to love it."

We actually hung out on many weekends at Mama's, letting our children play with their grandparents, as we talked about the thrill of our jobs. Needless to say, he had much more to talk about than I did.

A year passed and still there was no word—no request for an interview—even though I had a stellar record from childhood, through the military, and now into my corrections career.

One night, Officer Willie Polite called me. It was nearly midnight.

He said, "Anthony! I made my first arrest!"

Just a few months earlier, Willie had been a corrections officer serving with me. Now he was a Chatham County Police Officer—still under the care of his training officer and loving every minute of it.

Without leaving an opportunity for me to ask, he continued, "It was a DUI (driving under the influence of drugs or alcohol). Man, this guy was weaving all over the place. He was DANGEROUS and we needed to get him off the road before he killed somebody."

Willie was so hyped up that I just let him roll. "This man barely knew who he was or where he was going. But, he knew one thing. He knew he didn't want handcuffs."

He continued, "He bucked like a bronco when he felt that steel snap on his wrist. We had to hold him down. We got him in the car just like you see on TV and then we took him off to jail."

I said, "Man, you call me at 11:30 at night to tell me you got a drunk driver? What's wrong with you, man?"

We both had a good laugh. Oh, how I wanted to be in his shoes, doing work that really mattered. Instead, the next day he'd be out chasing down more drunks, or investigating burglaries, or finding a missing child. I, on the other hand, would be locked in the facility guarding and protecting "his" drunk.

Who else's chain could I rattle? Who else did I know who was now a police officer? Tommie Simpson. Morally, she was straight as an arrow, fair and respectful to all, and someone you could count on to do the job well.

We pulled the same shift when she was a corrections officer and I think she admired me as much as I admired her. The guys jokingly called her the "Old Lady" because she was more than a decade older than many of us.

Tommie appreciated a good sense of humor. When we worked together, it made the sentence—I mean, shift—go faster!

At the next opportunity, I called her.

"How do you like your job?" I asked. Then, I listened patiently as she told me about how she was doing everything that I wanted to be doing.

Finally, she countered, "How are you doing?"

I said, "I want to be where you are. You know nothing really changes around here."

"I know," she said empathetically. "The corrections center is like a revolving door. Pretty soon you realize you're seeing the same faces over and over again. But you kept it fun, Anthony. I really enjoyed working with you."

"I know," I agreed. But I'm not having fun here anymore. I'm ready to move on. I really, really want to be a police officer."

"I know," she said compassionately, "and I know your application is on file. They just aren't looking at it."

After a few more minutes, I lightened the tone and we ended the call with a laugh. Then, without telling me, Tommie Simpson mentioned me to her supervisor at the Chatham County Police Department.

Later, she told me, "I told my supervisor that we worked together for over two years. You got along with everyone, did a good job, and have a great sense of humor. I felt like you would be an asset to the department."

A few weeks later, I got the call I'd been waiting for. A face-to-face interview was scheduled. If memory serves, seven high-ranking officers grilled me with every possible question to determine if I would be an asset or a liability to the department.

The judgement fell in my favor. I was elated! I called Red. I called my brother. I called Tommie Simpson. I called everyone. I also sent a hand written thank you card to all seven of the officers who participated in my interview.

Later, I was told that this had never been done before. It wasn't just a formality for me. I truly was grateful for the opportunity to speak from my heart about why I wanted to be a police officer. I was ready, willing, and able to serve and protect.

Officially, on October 25, 1995—after serving three years as a corrections officer—I was officially hired as a Chatham County Police Officer. With that came an immediate $5000 pay raise, badge #143 and an official uniform, a police car—a powerful Crown Victoria—and a sleek silver Smith & Wesson .45 mm handgun.

I felt like—Anthony Bryant to the rescue!

Of all the uniforms I wore—this was my favorite.

On October 25, 1995 I was hired as a Chatham County Police Office in Savannah, Georgia.

Chapter Twenty

The Uniform

No one could have prepared me for the power of the uniform. When I slipped it on, it was like putting on a Superman suit. A real one. One that lets you fly.

This is not a self-delusion. I don't know why, but people actually give you power when you are wearing a police uniform.

What's odd, is that a corrections officer's garb is very similar to the police uniform. But, people know the difference. One time, I pulled into a 7-Eleven convenience store behind a corrections officer and overheard two clerks.

"Hey, what's with all the police officers?" the younger one asked.

"He's not a police officer," the older clerk said, pointing to the corrections officer. Then she added, rather disparagingly, " He's *just* a corrections officer. He don't got no gun."

Then she pointed proudly to me and announced, "He's a police officer!"

I tipped my hat and smiled broadly. Oh, yes I was and I was ready to save the day. When I walked in the store, I was offered free soda and snacks. That never happened when I was wearing a corrections uniform for three long years.

One evening, I pulled into that same 7-Eleven store to get a snack. As I approached the door, I saw a big man arguing with the clerk. As soon as I opened the door, the angry man's buddy tapped him on the shoulder and whispered, "It's the police."

You would have thought that someone waved a magic wand and instantly transformed this big brute into a kindhearted

Southern gentleman. Immediately, his angry snarl turned upward into a gentle grin and he said, "Good evening officer."

I nodded politely as I collected my free soda. I also collected my thoughts. Wow! What power! I just witnessed the Incredible Hulk turn into Mr. Rogers from Mr. Roger's Neighborhood. All I had to do was walk in—with this uniform—and things changed. I felt like I was standing on top of the world.

"Wow," I thought. "I LOVE this job in all caps!"

Then I swooped in for the rescue.

Looking the clerk directly in the eyes, I asked, "Is everything okay here?"

Relieved, she answered, "Sir, this man's come up here several times today trying to make trouble for me. Can you ask him to leave?"

Most likely, he was a former boyfriend or a wanna-be boyfriend. But it didn't make any difference to me. He had no right harassing her at work.

"Sir," I said firmly, yet respectfully, "you'll have to leave. You can leave immediately—peacefully—or I will arrest you for trespassing."

I then went on to explain that businesses have the right to ask customers or anyone to leave their property. If a person refuses to leave—by law he or she is trespassing. The man chose to leave.

My uniform also awarded me the best seats at the movie theater—and free tickets! In fact, when I would go to the show with Red, the manager would see me waiting in line, call me inside, and treat me like a celebrity.

"Officer Bryant, how are you? Come inside. You don't have to wait in line. Where would you like to sit?"

He recognized me and honored me whether I was in the uniform or not. It was a wonderful feeling.

I know that there is a saying: There are no free lunches in life. But that is simply not true for police officers. I ate a free lunch nearly every day. Fast food restaurants were happy to give uniformed officers complimentary meals just for stopping in. Popeye's Chicken was one of my favorites. I "made police presence known" at that delicious pit stop two or three times a week.

Even our fine dining restaurants gave us a hefty discount. Restaurants such as Pearl's Saltwater Grille –on La Roche Avenue—right on the waterfront, took 50% off the bill. I couldn't get enough of their fantail shrimp, fried oysters, New York Strip, or fresh catch of the day. I mean, this was (and still is) melt in your mouth—true taste of the South cooking. I ate there so often, the staff knew me by name.

But, I soon found out that there was also a dark side to the uniform. It was a magnet for women. Now I don't mean cheap, low-living, uneducated females. This uniform attracted highly sophisticated women—even married women—with multiple degrees and all the good looks that money could buy.

Apparently, when they looked at the uniform—with tan shirt, gold badge, dark brown pants, belt, campaign hat, and gun—they saw what I felt. They saw Superman.

Now if I was a single guy, this unwanted attention may have been a good thing. But as it was, I was married to Red and up to this point, I was 100% committed to our marriage.

Now, temptation was calling my name on a daily basis. Even Officer Tommie Osborne—one of the most conservative police officers that I know—told me, "I don't know what it is. Something about that uniform causes people to throw themselves at you. Men ask me out all the time."

She added, "The first thing I tell them is, 'I'm married.'"

The other vice that it attracts is lawbreaking. When you think about it, it only makes sense. The best way to protect an illegal activity is to hire a uniform to guard it. So officers have opportunities galore to run a side "business"—thereby doubling their income.

I believe that few new officers would ever succumb to the temptation. But when it is offered over and over again, it can be a matter of time before the right person—someone you trust—makes the proposition.

Chapter Twenty-One

Directing Traffic

"Chatham to 143," the dispatcher radioed.

"Go ahead," I replied.

"Respond to the Ogeechee Road and Chatham Parkway intersection . The traffic light is out. Need traffic assistance."

"On my way," I said calmly. But inside, I was excited and nervous. This was my first day cut loose from my training officer and I was alone in my patrol car. I wanted to do this right. Done wrong, I could actually cause an accident.

On my way to the intersection, I replayed in my mind the one time that I'd directed traffic alongside my trainer. Lt. Jeff Olson was really good at it. His movements were crisp, his rhythm was smooth, and traffic flowed easily.

Lt. Jeff Olson was an excellent trainer.

He later became commander of the Hostage Negotiation Team (SWAT)

Hoping for the best, I parked my car and watched the traffic for a moment. Cars from all sides were cautiously proceeding through the intersection in a haphazard way. Clearly, help was needed.

I walked to the center of the intersection, extended my right arm with palm up and blew my whistle.

All cars stopped.

I positioned my shoulders parallel to the traffic that I was about to signal to move. Next, I made eye contact with the first driver in the Northbound lane and signaled him to proceed. As soon as that lane was moving, I signaled the Southbound lane to join in.

After mentally approximating the length of a signal, I stopped the North/South traffic with palm extended toward the cars. Next, I signaled for the left turns. Once the turn lanes were empty, I bent my arm from the elbow—palm up to motion the Eastbound traffic to move. Then, as before, I signaled for the Westbound lane to join in.

In short order, I found my rhythm. I was actually moving traffic—just like a seasoned officer. No one knew that this was my first time and no one cared. Instead, when I put my palm up—traffic stopped. Even the 18-wheelers. Everyone was respecting my commands.

Suddenly, I felt like I had the keys to the world. People were relying on me to get them to their destinations safely and I was making it happen.

As I continued to direct traffic a feeling of pride continued to well up in me. I had to laugh. This was so much more FUN than sitting in a corrections center. I was doing something real. People were responding to my help and nodding in thanks.

As I basked in that feeling, I thought, "Oh my gosh! Even the birds and the airplanes stop when I raise my hand."

Does it get any better than this?

Chapter Twenty-Two

First Arrest

I have to say that I was a bit hardcore in my first twelve months on duty. Considerable power had been vested in this 28-year-old officer and I wanted to do my upmost to keep the community safe and served.

So when problems didn't jump out at me, I went looking for them. I remember one time, a man had his license plate hanging on by just one screw. It looked like it was about ready to fall off his vehicle.

Instead of pulling up beside him at a stop light and saying, "Sir, you need to fix your license plate," I flipped on my lights and the siren and pulled him over.

"Sir, I'm going to need to see your driver's license and proof of registration."

As I walked back to my car—that powerful Crown Victoria with blue lights flashing—I thought of Knight Rider.

In an instant, I was transported back to my childhood living room in the 1980s watching my favorite show.

I replayed the famous intro silently in my mind.

Old school techno music repeats "da-da, da-da da-da, da-da, dada" as a pin dot of a car speeds toward the camera.

Then a strong, manly voice announces, "Knight Rider. A shadowy flight into the dangerous world of a man who does not exist."

The pitch black K.I.T.T. car—with strobing red grill lights—speeds toward the camera. Voice fades as the backbeat amps up. The camera pans a view of the colorful digital dashboard.

Then, star David Hasslehoff jumps out of his car and flashes a winning smile as the mystery voice says, "Michael Knight. A young loner on a crusade to champion the cause of the innocent, the helpless, the powerless—in a world of criminals who operate above the law."

Michael taps the Turbo Boost button and the K.I.T.T. car blasts into the air.

Man, I am living my dream. No. That's not true.

When I was a young black man—living in the projects in the 1980s—I never dreamed that this life was possible for me. I'm living beyond my dream!

Oh. Back to reality. I've got a guy with a tired tag hanging off his bumper. I called his information in—mandatory for anyone who is pulled over—and he came out clean as a choir girl.

As I returned his documents, I said, "All right, Sir. Just take care of your tag and everything will be fine."

My first big catch came a couple days later.

"Chatham to 143," the dispatcher radioed.

"Go ahead," I replied.

"Respond to a domestic call...."

I was there in a red hot minute—lights and siren blaring. These calls can be dangerous because emotions are high and anger is present. Plus, many folks have guns in the house.

"What seems to be the problem, Ma'am?" I asked.

Before she could answer, the guy butted in and started talking. I decided to go with it and let him talk.

After he stated his case, I turned to look at the woman and asked, "Okay, Ma'am. Would you like to tell me what happened?"

She said three words and he yelled, "That's a lie! That is not what happened."

I said, "Sir, I let you talk. Let's let the lady have her say. I need you to keep quiet."

His shoulders dropped and he said, "Okay."

Then she said about three more words. He stood up taller and threw his hands up yelling, "That's a lie! You KNOW that's a lie!"

This happened three times. The guy just would not shut up and let her talk. He had no respect for the woman and no respect for the uniform. So I finally said, "Sir, if I have to tell you one more time to be quiet so she can talk, then I'm going to arrest you for disorderly conduct in addition to the domestic violence charge. Do I make myself clear?"

He said, "Yes."

And it happened again!

I said, "Sir, you are under arrest for disorderly conduct by refusing to obey an officer and on the domestic violence charge."

That got his attention. He pleaded, "Please. Please. I promise I won't say another word. I'll let her talk. I'm sorry. I'm sorry."

"It's too late," I told him. "Once I give my word, I never go back on it. You are under arrest."

He cooperated as I put on the handcuffs. Then, I led him to the car quietly. And yes—just like in the movies—I protected his head as he moved into the back seat.

Then I read him his Miranda Rights.

"You have the right to remain silent. Anything you say can and will be used against you in a court of law. You have the right to an attorney. If you cannot afford an attorney, one will be provided for you. Do you understand the rights I have just read to you? With these rights in mind, do you wish to speak to me?"

After I drove him to jail—I felt a little rush. It's kind of like a guy shooting his first buck. But this was like a two-point spike horn. Not too impressive, but better than coming home with an empty tag.

That night, I continued to replay the event in my mind. Would I do anything differently? I don't think so. I needed to protect the woman. If the man couldn't even control himself with an armed and uniformed police officer in his house—then her call for help was probably urgent.

I concluded that if I had a chance to rewind, I would not change a thing.

Chapter Twenty-Three

Big Buck

Police don't wait for dispatch to call. We "patrol" our assigned neighborhood—keeping our eyes and ears on high alert.

We ask ourselves, "What's out of place? Who's acting suspicious?" It is this hypervigilant state (elevated awareness in search of potential hazards) that keeps us alive. It's called "police safety." Law officers never want to be caught unaware. It could cost them their lives.

Because of this—and our oath to serve and protect—we guard our assigned turf just like we'd guard our own home and family.

One late Saturday night, I saw a car swerving on the road. Immediately, the hairs on the back of my neck stood up.

"You're on my road, drunk?" I said to myself as I flipped on the lights and approached the car.

"Not on my watch, buddy!"

Officers get that mentality. We take it personally. I actually felt personally violated by this driver who was endangering the lives of innocent people.

The last thing I wanted was a morning headline that read, *Drunk Driver Kills Four,* on my turf during my duty.

I waited for backup—another safety measure that is equally important as a bullet proof vest—and then approached the car.

"Sir, I'll need to see your driver's license and proof of registration."

As he fumbled around, I asked, "Sir, have you been drinking?"

Without waiting for him to answer, I ordered, "Sir, I need you to step out of the car."

Everything went smoothly, until I snapped on the first cuff. It was like he suddenly snapped out of his alcohol-induced stupor—now fully aware that he was going to jail.

"No!" he protested as he pushed away.

But I was ready for him. Though I'm not a big guy, I could easily pin him against the car to snap on the other cuff.

Now this was a big buck arrest. It came with an equally big adrenaline rush. I really had taken a "bad guy" off the road and kept my citizens safe. This had to be a 12-point buck.

Chapter Twenty-Four

My Gun

My gun was my baby. I cleaned it, dressed it up with a custom pistol grip, and—as a lefty—kept it firmly secured on my left side.

This sleek, silver, Smith & Wesson 45mm could mean the difference between life and death. Like all law officers—my first priority was to make sure that I made it home every night. In that way, I could go to work—to serve and protect—again in the morning.

Our weapon is such an important part of our safety that we refused to work with an officer who could not shoot well. In fact, a candidate for the Academy cannot become a sworn officer without qualifying with his or her weapon.

Each year, we qualify again. If for some reason, a seasoned officer fails to qualify, that officer will receive remedial training until the problem is remedied. If the issue can't be fixed, the officer is taken off the streets.

There are three levels of weapon competence— marksman, sharp shooter, and expert. I'm better than average— a strong sharp shooter.

Oh, and just to clarify, officers—like military personnel—are trained to shoot for center of mass. Our mission is to stop the dangerous person. We are never trained to shoot someone in the arm or the leg to slow them down or disable them.

Using our weapon is a split-second decision and shooting at center of mass (the chest) is trained in so deeply that it becomes a reflex response.

Interestingly, I never shot my gun in the line of duty during my entire career as a Chatham County Police Officer. However, I did have it drawn and ready to shoot on many occasions.

One time, I was called to a burglary.

"Chatham to 143," the dispatcher radioed.

"Go ahead," I replied.

"Respond to a reported burglary at Westlake Avenue..."

My heart raced. Talk about my turf—that is the neighborhood where I grew up. I flipped on the lights and let the siren scream. It seemed like pure adrenaline was speeding through my veins.

My thoughts raced as I realized that City police also covered this area. Maybe my brother Tommy was also responding to this call. Imagine, two brothers in the hood coming to save the day.

When I came to within a mile of the apartments, I shut down the lights and the noise. There was no sense in alerting the burglar. Our goal was to catch him in the building so we could get him off the streets.

I waited until back up arrived. All the while I was thinking that someone was breaking into MY home. I was here to defend THIS home just like it was MY home. This was MY turf and someone had the arrogance to break into a house on my watch. Not going to happen!

My job was to make sure that everyone knew that I was the baddest thing here on this side of town from 3 p.m. to 11 p.m. If anything happened, I better know about it and I WOULD take care of it.

Back up arrived in less than a minute. We were all out with weapons drawn. Someone motioned for me to walk to the back of the property. The other officers covered the other sides of the building. We were hoping to flush the burglar out and make an arrest.

Once again, nothing happened. A neighbor had called, reporting that someone climbed in the back window. But I didn't see any signs of forced entry. We called dispatch and cleared the call.

Another time, I was patrolling the business district. The front door was slightly open, even though it was well after business hours. I called for backup and we went in with guns drawn.

"Police!" I yelled as I pushed open the door.

Keeping my gun out at arm's length and eye level, we searched the building for burglars or vagrants.

Each corner we rounded, we called out, "Police!"

No response. No movement. Nothing at all.

I had the dispatcher call the business owner. His wife drove him to the shop. He showed up a bit tipsy. Probably too snockered to remember to close and lock his own front door

Both Sides of the Bars

Chapter Twenty-Five

High Speed Chase

One of the most exciting days in my career happened at 8:17 p.m. on May 23, 1997. I pulled over a vehicle with a dealer's tag hanging off the bumper. My intention was to ask him to fix the tag.

"Good evening," I said as I approached the car.

Before I even had time to request his driver's license, the man stomped on the gas and sped off.

I ran back to my car and slammed the gearshift into drive.

"143 Chatham County, I'm in a 1080 (code for car chase). I'm heading east on I-16."

There was a long beep, clearing the channel. This alert lets everyone know that something big is happening. It could be an officer down, or a burglary in progress. Everyone listens for more information.

As I raced in pursuit—lights flashing and siren screaming—my thoughts whirled. Was this a kidnapping? Did the driver have a warrant out for a murder? Why did he run? What does he have to hide? Does he have a gun? What about his passenger? Is he armed and dangerous?

My supervisor, Sgt. Nichols, came on the line.

"Where are you?" he asked.

After giving him my location, he said, "All other units—stay out of it."

He directed his next comment to me. "I'm headed toward you. Do you copy? 10-4."

"10-4." I replied.

In a volley of conversation, the assistant supervisor in the dispatcher's office and my supervisor on the road concluded that the green Nissan pickup was likely a code 41 (stolen vehicle). I was advised to continue the pursuit.

As I was flying down the road—sometimes upwards of 100 m.p.h—it was like a scene out of a movie. Cars were pulling off the road and letting me pass, but the suspect was driving like a wild man.

Then the suspect proceeded to drive the wrong way on Talmadge Memorial Bridge forcing other drivers off the road.

In the meantime, dispatch had alerted the South Carolina police as the suspected headed toward the state line. They put down strips so that if the suspect continued beyond the bridge, his tires would burst.

By this time, Georgia State Trooper B.H. Stickland had joined the chase. His Mustang—faster and meaner than my car—took over the pursuit.

I advised my supervisors that I crossed the first bridge and was about to cross the second bridge—into South Carolina. Entering another jurisdiction requires permission, but I was giving constant updates and continually told, "10-4."

"Chatham, I just crossed the South Carolina state line."

My supervisor said, "10-4. You are advised to continue with the 1080. 10-4."

"10-4," I replied.

When the suspect saw the line of police cars on the other side of the bridge—he immediately slammed on the breaks, stopped his truck, and ran on foot into the woods. His passenger rolled out of the car and laid on the ground with his hands up.

I held my gun on the passenger as I watched Officer Strickland—a heavy set guy—run after him.

Suddenly, I heard, "Boom! Boom!" Officer Strickland fired two warning shots. Then he yelled, "Police! Stop or I'll shoot!"

That was the end of the chase.

Together, Officer Strickland and I cuffed the two suspects. Then they were hauled off to jail in South Carolina. Later, they were brought back to Georgia for trial.

When the chase was done, my mind kept racing. I finally got back to the office at 11 p.m. My shift was over. I replayed the chase for my fellow officers and then settled in to write the lengthy report.

As a side note, most people don't realize that when a police shift ends, so does the pay. So the two hours of paperwork I did was an expected freebee.

When I finally arrived at home, Red was already asleep. She had to work in the morning and had been running after kids all evening. So I knew better than to wake her to share my news.

But I had to share it with someone. Even several hours later, I felt like I'd just run a marathon. Exhausted as I was, my heart was still racing and my mind was wide awake. So I talked it over with my new best friend, Budweiser.

It was just me and Budweiser, sitting in the big chair changing channels on the television. In a few hours, I was finally numb enough to entertain the idea of sleep.

The next day, my picture was in the *Savannah Morning News*. Photographer Bob Morris captured the moment when Officer Strickland and I were cuffing the suspect. But, my glory was short lived.

COASTAL EMPIRE

May 1997

HIGH-SPEED CHASE

Georgia State Patrol trooper B.H. Strickland and Chatham County police officer A.K. Bryant arrest a suspect in a chase Friday night that started in Savannah and ended in South Carolina. The vehicle sped off after Bryant stopped it at Ogeechee Road and Interstate 516. The chase went from there to I-16 and over the Talmadge Memorial Bridge into Jasper County, where the driver drove the wrong way and ran other motorists off the road before stopping. After a foot chase through woods, officers charged driver Jonathan Sapp, 20, of Savannah and his passenger, Keith Metzger, 22, of Savannah with fleeing and attempting to elude police and reckless driving. Sapp also has been charged with driving with a suspended license. Both are being held in a South Carolina. Chatham County officials will obtain warrants for the men on Tuesday, Bryant said.

An investigation determined that I should not have crossed the state line. In fact, I should not have continued the pursuit because clearly the suspect was endangering the lives of innocent people in the high speed chase. I should have disengaged and perhaps the suspect would have slowed down.

I fought back. "I was following protocol," I insisted. "There were two supervisors overseeing the chase and I was told to continue."

It didn't matter. My supervisor, Sgt. Nichols, was given two weeks off work with no pay. I was given a week off with no pay. Georgia State Patrol Trooper Stickland was reprimanded by his agency for shooting into the air. He made that decision to shorten the chase. However, it is against regulations for officers to fire warning shots.

And guess what the suspect was running from? He was driving illegally—with a suspended license and he had a small marijuana cigarette in his possession. Both of those are misdemeanor offenses. I left his name out of this book because the kid was only 20. Today, he's probably 40 years old, still wondering: What was I thinking?

Both Sides of the Bars

Chapter Twenty-Six

Excessive Force

Everything I've written is true—but it's only half the story of police work. Now I'm going to tell the other half, so readers can understand *why* police work is controversial and rife with compromise and corruption.

Going back to Basic Law Enforcement Academy, I was taught the *ideal*. Police officers are emotionally balanced, moral giants who defend the defenseless and maintain law and order.

Once candidates are sworn in, they receive three-weeks of on the job training. A role model officer with plenty of experience partners with the new officer.

My trainer was awesome. Sgt. Jeff Olson was the personification of professionalism and command presence. In fact, he eventually became commander of the Hostage Negotiation Team for the Chatham County Police Department.

When he arrived on the scene—all eyes were on him. He quickly took control of the situation and determined the cause of the problem. He could stand his ground regardless of public opinion.

His mind was on high alert, scanning words and movements for clues of what was about to unfold. And he had the ability to suppress his feelings so that his thoughts could rule while on duty. That is called COMMAND PRESENCE and he had it down pat.

He handled 99% of the calls we responded to by the book. When the school was broken into, we went in, made our observations, and filed our reports. It was fast. It was easy. It was done. When the traffic light blew out, we centered ourselves, gave signals, and kept traffic flowing.

However, on two occasions during my 3-week training, Sgt. Olson used excessive force—by my definition. On the first occasion, we were called to shut down a loud party. The neighbor placed the call.

It happened to be the home of a firefighter. When we arrived the firefighter said, "Hey, man. What's the big deal? We're just having a little party."

I'm sure his intention was to save face and be cool in front of his drinking buddies. But, Officer Olson wasn't there to negotiate.

"You need to shut this party down. Someone called in and complained," Officer Olson said sternly.

"I don't understand...," the man began.

In mid-sentence, Officer Olson grabbed his wrist and shoved him to the ground. I never saw that coming and was a bit shocked. However, I kept silent and watched.

The party was shut down, but the next day we were called in by Internal Affairs. The investigators plopped down pictures of the firefighter's wrist bearing unmistakable evidence that force was used. The bruises were deep and dark.

Officer Olson claimed that he used the force necessary to obtain compliance with the law. Then, the investigators turned and looked at me.

"What happened?" they asked.

Now I thought to myself, "What am I supposed to do?" Sgt. Olson is my trainer. He is holding my career in his hands. *If I snitch, my career is over.*

And if I ask for another trainer, Sgt. Olson will inform the new trainer and he will make it twice as hard for me. I knew this much from being in the military. It never pays to go against your superior.

I also knew that officers have to make split-second decisions. Things can escalate from domestic disturbance to someone pulling a gun and ordering an officer down in a matter of seconds. Maybe the lead officer—the more experienced officer—saw something I didn't see. After all, we were in a room full of people under the influence of alcohol and some of them likely had weapons.

Just like in the military, you let each team member make their own call, and then you talk it out after the fact. But during the battle—or the call—you stand together and cover each other's backs. This simple rule—the bond, the loyalty—is a MUST for police safety.

And, in fact, my trainer and I did talk about this when we returned to our vehicle.

I asked, "Why didn't we talk it out with the man? Why didn't we reason with him?"

Officer Olson said, "We don't have time for that. He knew what he needed to do."

With that, we were off to the next call. Actually, we had a whole list of backed up calls. Nothing was urgent, but when I make a call—I want attention. It all ends up being urgent to the person calling for help.

The investigators asked me again, "Officer Bryant, What happened?"

I simply raised my eyebrows, slowly shook my head, and said, "There was a whole lot of drinking going on. He did what he had to do."

Basically, I lied.

As we walked out of the room, Officer Olson smiled at me, as if to say, "Anthony, you're all right. You covered for me and down the line, you might need someone to cover for you. You're going to do just fine."

There were other considerations too. Let's say that I snitched and the firefighter sued the agency. He could say that when he was thrown down, he hit his head. Now, every time he hears a police siren he gets traumatized. That would cost our department money—money that could be used for new patrol cars, new technology, or new uniforms. So I was not stepping on the ant hill.

Then, there are the long-term ramifications of being a snitch. In shorthand: No one wants to work with you. If no one will work with you, you are out of a job. Even if you do keep your job, your chances of promotion are nearly non-existent. Let's say you want to transfer to K-9, or the D.A.R.E. program, or the Marine program.

The commander in charge is going to ask my supervisor, "Hey, how is Anthony? He put in for K-9."

My supervisor is going to say, "He's a square. You can't trust him."

Deal done. No promotion. Upward mobility is dead.

The second time I witnessed excessive force happened when we were called to arrest a man with outstanding warrants.

We knocked on the trailer door, and when the man realized we were going to arrest him, he bolted out the back door.

We ran after him. Off to the side was a barking German Shepherd that was restrained on a chain. It was no threat to us, but Officer Olson kicked it in the face.

Later, a woman called the department to file a complaint. It never went anywhere. She was "trailer trash" and didn't have a voice. Everyone knew that she couldn't afford an attorney to speak for her. So, the complaint was dismissed.

Did I agree with this? Absolutely not! I really felt bad for the dog and the woman. But, I was not about to get myself tangled up in this sticky web.

Even retired Officer Tommie Osborne recently told me, "When I was working as a detective, my partner and I went on a call as backup. A guy had a warrant for his arrest and he was already in cuffs when we arrived. Then, the male officer took the butt of a gun and hit the suspect in the face. We walked away."

"I said to my partner," Officer Osborne continued, "'We are not going to witness that.' Supervisors were out there too. We didn't volunteer anything."

Her rule of thumb: "You have to learn not to see."

Both Sides of the Bars

Chapter Twenty-Seven

Racism

My trainer—Sgt. Jeff Olson—was white. In all our time together, I never saw any evidence of racism. However, I did have the race card pulled on me.

One time I was tailing a drunk driver when he pulled into a supermarket parking lot. I pulled up behind him and called for backup.

It just so happened that "old lady"—Officer Tommie Osborne—was my partner that night. When she arrived, we approached the car.

"Sir," I said, "I'm going to need to see your driver's license and proof of insurance."

He said, "Officer, I just want to go in to buy a case of beer. I'm not hurting anyone."

"Sir," I replied, " you are drunk. I can't allow you to buy any alcohol. In fact, I've been following you for several blocks now and you are swerving all over the road. I'm going to have to arrest you for driving under the influence."

"What!" slurred the white man. "I'm not drunk. You're arresting me because I'm white. You're a racist."

"No Sir," I countered. "My job is to keep the roads safe and you have been driving drunk. I'll need you to step out of your car."

"I'm not going anywhere. I want to talk to your supervisor," he insisted.

So we called in his request. And, wouldn't you know, the supervisor on duty was black. So now, he had three black officers putting him under arrest.

When his complaint of racism was investigated by Internal Affairs, it was determined that—white or black—he was drunk. His arrest was appropriate and no racism was involved.

Our goal was simply to get a drunk off the streets before he killed himself or someone else. He was playing the race card, but it didn't work.

On another occasion, I responded to a domestic dispute in a very beautiful neighborhood. The man—a doctor—must have lived in a million dollar house.

When he opened the door, he looked me up and down contemptuously. Then he said, "No black man is stepping into my house."

I calmly replied, "Sir, I'm Officer Anthony Bryant and I'm responding to a call your wife made."

He barely let me in and he was so arrogant and racist that I had every right to arrest him. Not only did he clearly slap his wife—to the point that she had a nose bleed—but he was refusing to obey an officer.

In the end, I decided to err on the side of mercy. He said that she slapped him first and he did have evidence of having been hit. I could have arrested both of them for domestic violence. Instead, I asked if one of them could spend the night in a hotel or with a friend until they each had a chance to cool off.

That was agreeable to both of them. The husband packed a small bag and left for the night.

The incident watered a little seed of cynicism. It was beginning to look like everyone—even the people who looked like they had it all together—were messed up. My idealism began to be replaced by pessimism and distrust.

Both Sides of the Bars

Chapter Twenty-Eight

First Compromise

In my experience, a police force operates much like a gang. To get in, you have to break a law. Only then, does the group know that you can be trusted. The logic is quite simple. Now we have dirt on you. So if you turn us in, we will turn you in.

On the flip side, it means—I'll cover for you and you will cover for me. In police lingo it is called "cloaking."

***Cloaking** means that at most, you will lie for me. At the very least, if someone questions you about my actions you will feign ignorance.*

The standard response: "I don't know what you are talking about."

Now for a *new* officer, the number one priority is to gain the trust of his fellow officers. They want to know that you are not afraid to fight, that they can count on you to carry your load, and that you will watch their backs.

It is extremely difficult—a multi-month process—to prove that you are trustworthy. It's also a lonely time—because they are not letting you in. More than a few recruits quit—never earning entrance into the club.

My first test came shortly after I was hired. Department policy mandates no alcohol be consumed for eight hours prior to reporting for duty. About 4 o'clock one afternoon, I got a call from one of the officers assigned to my shift.

"Anthony," he said, "why don't you stop over at about 6 o'clock. I'm grilling some burgers. We'll get a chance to talk before our shift."

"Hotdog!" I thought silently to myself. My first invitation to hang out with the officers. I quickly confirmed.

After I arrived, we bantered a bit about sports, and everyday news. Then, at about 7 o'clock, he got up and popped open a beer. He looked me right in the eye and took a drink. Then he popped the top off a second beer and held it up for me.

What am I supposed to do?

I just witnessed an officer breaking department policy. We have to report for duty in four hours.

If I refuse the beer, I will likely be ostracized. I won't be invited to any more cookouts.

I don't want people to think I'm the Lone Ranger. I want to be accepted as part of the team. Actually, I *need* to be accepted as part of the team. Police work is too dangerous without impeccable trust between the officers. Besides, if he can't trust me, he will think that I might "flip on him" and turn him in if any incidents come up in the future.

So, I smiled broadly, extended my hand and accepted the beer. At 11 o'clock that evening, we were sitting in the briefing room. He smiled at me and nodded. I'd passed the first test.

Both Sides of the Bars

Chapter Twenty-Nine

Adultery

In 1996, after having been a police officer for just a few months, the guys started pressuring me to have an affair. Well, maybe it wasn't pressure. They were tempting me.

By this time, I was getting invited to my fellow officers homes quite regularly. We either met when their wives were not home, or we went to the home of a bachelor.

Over beer and barbeque, the guys would begin to tell their hilarious stories.

"My girlfriend ran into my wife at the grocery store," one officer said.

"Oh my gosh. What did she do?"

"She helped her find the Teriyaki Sauce," he said as he slapped his knee.

The group laughed so hard we had tears streaming out of our eyes.

The officer continued, "My old lady didn't have a clue."

Another officer was busted. His wife found out about his affair, so now it was on the down low.

"I'm going to have to show my face around the house a little more often until this thing blows over," he said.

We all shook our heads in sympathy and shared a moment of silence. Then, someone told a new tale of adulterous adventure. As you might guess, it eventually came around to me.

Now, here was my dilemma. Red and I had been married for nearly nine years. We were 100% faithful to each other and frankly, though I was periodically tempted, I never had the heart to betray Red. Well, that is until I started hearing how fun and "normal" it was to have a girlfriend on the side.

I began to wonder if I was missing out on something. Now that I had the Superman uniform—maybe I deserved Superman privileges. After all, how many REAL men sleep with only one woman in their entire lifetime. Maybe I needed to try some new flavors.

If my out-of-control ego was not enough to send me over the edge of adultery—my shift officers were there to help. It was another case of upping the ante. Sure, I'd compromised on the beer. But, was I willing to put the family of officers first— even ahead of Red and the two children?

At first I hedged by bluffing. I told them of my fantasies—the beautiful women in Germany.

"Oh my gosh," I gushed, "These women were so beautiful. They looked like models you'd see in a magazine. One of the women—a redhead—started hanging around the post and frankly, she didn't care if I was black or red or green."

Those fantasy affairs bought me some time, but eventually the group demanded that I put my money where my mouth was. One day, they cornered me at a barbecue and told me that a lady in the Sheriff's Department was asking about me.

One of my buddies said, "She asked me, 'Who's that stud?'"

My other buddy chimed in, "She's interested in you man. What are you going to do?"

I was nervous. I thought about Red. She was my high school sweetheart. I'd known her since I was 16. In all this time, she'd been my best friend, and confidant. In the past nine years, she'd matured into the most phenomenal woman and mother of our children.

Here I sat, at the crossroads of decision. Who did I value most: Red or my fellow officers? And then, I realized that without really perceiving it, I'd been drifting farther and farther away from Red with each barbeque and bar stop after work. Between my rotating shifts, off-duty work, and a little mentoring I did at a local school—I wasn't home much at all.

"Give her my telephone number," I told them with a smile.

Two days later, she called me. As our conversations increased, so did my confidence. Finally, the big day arrived. Yes. We had sex. No. It wasn't good. So, we did it again and again and it got better.

This experience armed me with real tales to tell. Now my buddies knew that I was all in. I had just risked my family for my fellow officers. I would cloak for them and they would cloak for me.

A few weeks later, while I was in the shower, my cell phone buzzed. Red picked it up. She noticed that the text was from a female. By the time I turned off the water, she'd read enough messages to know that I'd been unfaithful.

"Who's _____?" she demanded with tears streaming down her face.

"She's just a friend, someone from work," I said, unaware that she already knew.

"Don't lie to me!"

"Oh, Baby." I went to hold her and she pushed me away, pounding on my chest.

"How could you do this to US?"

I felt her pain—the broken trust. Suddenly, I cared more about Red. What had I done?

"It was meant for you to pick up my phone. I shouldn't have done what I did. I'm sorry. I needed to get caught. I will never do that again," I promised.

But I did. Adultery is addictive. It is what so many police officers do because it's a power trip. It is something to brag about.

Police culture is known to be glutted with alcohol and adultery. Actually, a lot of officers have a girlfriend—or boyfriend if they are a female or a rare homosexual—on each side of town so that they always have someone on the line no matter where they are assigned.

There's also a bit of competition.

We used to compete to see how many phone numbers from females we could collect in a week. Some officers took it up a notch to see how many women they could get under their belt in 30 days. But really, this was easy. Women were throwing themselves at us all the time.

My second affair began when I saw a beautiful woman standing at the grocery store. She smiled and introduced herself. I smiled back and we had a brief conversation. Before we parted ways, we traded phone numbers.

All was well, until she wanted more of me. When I couldn't give her all my off-duty time, she sabotaged both of my relationships—the one with her and the one with Red. Here is how it happened.

One day, while I was in the briefing room, preparing for my 3 p.m. shift, the voice on the loud speaker said, "Officer Bryant, you have a telephone call in the lobby."

This was pretty common because people call about their police reports or tickets. So I immediately left to take the call. When I answered, it was my former girlfriend.

"Anthony," she said in her most seductive voice, "I miss you. Remember how much fun we had together. I really want you back. Can we please get back together?"

She then went on to retell one of our most memorable sexual encounters, while begging for a chance to do it again.

What's a guy to do? I'm a hero—and here was a damsel in distress, so I said, "Sure Baby. I'll make it happen real soon. Let me call you back a little later."

There was a moment of silence. Then I heard a different voice on the phone. It was a voice that I'd known since I was 16 years old. It was Red.

She screamed, "Anthony—you did what?"

It may as well have been the voice of God himself. It was like lightning striking my chest and stopping my heart. I couldn't talk. I couldn't breathe. I couldn't believe my ears.

It was only then that I realized that my former girlfriend placed a three-way call—letting Red hear the whole story first hand.

After I recovered, I thought to myself, "Man, I'm just not very good at this. How is it that some of my buddies have been doing this for years without getting caught and I'm getting caught every time."

Of course, at the next barbeque, my buddies thought this was hilarious. It did make a good story, telling blow by blow how it all went down. But on the serious side, I knew that I was ruining my marriage. I lied to myself and told myself that when things settled down, I would begin spending more time with Red and the children.

But police work never settled down. It was never boring. I LOVED my job. Every day was different. And I was developing quite an appetite for alcohol—my nightly friend—and the addictive excitement of adultery. Before I knew it, my whole life centered on me, me, me.

My last affair was with a cheerleader from school. We'd always admired each other in high school, but I had Red and she had her boyfriend. So we were just admirers.

Then one day, I saw her at the gas pump. She'd maintained her awesome cheerleader good looks and I didn't look half bad in my Superman uniform. We flirted a bit—testing the waters—and then we dove right in.

At the time of my arrest, I was about ready to terminate our relationship because she too was wanting too much of me. I didn't have any intention of breaking up my family or replacing Red. I wanted to stay married with the fringe benefits of being free and philandering

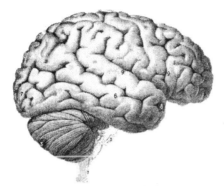

By this time, the power and prestige of being a police officer had totally hijacked my 28-year-old brain.

Now on the flip side—I absolutely did not want Red to have an affair. So I was very careful to keep the excitement alive in our sex life. Additionally, I bought her gifts, took her out on dates, and gave her the "words of endearment" that every woman longs to hear.

But in my Superman mode, I also developed some faulty thinking that shocks me now. Somehow, I convinced myself that when I was committing adultery with a married woman, I was actually *saving* her marriage.

I was adding excitement into her boring marriage—so that she could go on being married to the slug that was out there knocking himself out to keep her cozy in their oversized lifestyle. I had a great sense of humor too. I kept these women laughing and looking at the bright side of life. I was doing my duty. No...I was a hero!

As months passed, I became so egotistical that I stopped hiding my affairs. Instead of driving my girlfriends out of town, I took them to the same theater or restaurant where I took my wife.

I have to say in Red's defense, that she really did care. One time, she spoke to a bachelor officer friend of mine and pleaded with him.

"Please don't lead Anthony down this path," she said with tears in her eyes.

"Anthony is a good man. He's a good father," she added.

He was a good friend. He cloaked for me. He said, "I don't know what you're talking about."

At this point, when I met my brother Tommy, we had even more to talk about. Without knowing it, I was becoming more and more like him. I'd been cloaking for him for years—even before joining the force. Now, I knew *why* he had so many women. He was a thrill seeker and I was becoming one too.

One day, when we were engaging in a bragfest about our money, traffic stops, and girlfriends, Momma came in her living room. She opened her mouth, and out came the Bible. Very simply she said, "Watch out, boys. You may gain the world, but lose your soul." (Matthew 16:26)

Those words came back to haunt me about a year later.

Chapter Thirty

Play Along to Get Along

One night I pulled over a 17-year-old teenager for speeding. He wasn't just going 10 miles over the speed limit. He was using the road as his personal dragstrip.

Instead of getting the customary, "I'm sorry, officer"— he started cursing me!

"How *dare* you pull me over," he threatened. "Do you know who I am—you #*##!"

I didn't *care* who he was. He was endangering others and now he was disrespecting and refusing to obey an officer. So, I arrested him.

I took him down to get booked, but virtually before the ink could dry, his daddy was there to rescue him. Now, typically, a citizen cannot see the Judge until morning. So the very fact that his dad could get the Judge to pull some strings at 11 o'clock at night should have told me something.

The next thing I knew, I was being pulled in for questioning by my supervisor. It was like I was being asked to find a loophole—something I may have done wrong—so that the kid could get off scot-free.

I refused to incriminate myself. So, the department employed another tactic. They simply let it die. It never went to court.

I inquired one time and was told to drop it. Leave it alone.

I could have made a big stink and insisted that the teen be tried. However, that would have been a case of winning the war, but losing the battle.

The Chief didn't want the teen to go to court. The teen was the son of the man who owned the big car dealership—Backus Cadillac—in Savannah, Georgia. It was commonly believed that "daddy" gifted the Chief a new car. So, apparently, this is what the "gift" bought him.

Word was, he also gave the Mayor a "gift." I wondered what kind of favors it bought him from the town. It was "seeing the belly of society" that began to wring out every last drop of idealism from my young officer's heart.

I learned another thing too. Don't be a whistleblower. A friend took the time to explain the politics of the police department. Here's the way it works.

If I see an officer doing something illegal—I might be tempted to tell my supervisor. However, the officer doing wrong just might be drinking buddy of the Chief. The wrongdoer may be covering for the Chief's affairs with other women.

So when the Chief gets the report that new recruit Anthony Bryant is about to shut down the career of his good buddy—it's not the good buddy whose going down. It's Anthony Bryant. They would find some way to find me guilty of insubordination and squeeze me out. Then, my accusation would simply dry up and fly away.

Because there is so much corruption—you don't know WHO to tell. In the end, each officer has to decide whether to roll with the system or get out of the game. I stayed in.

Chapter Thirty-One

They Are All Crazy

It took exactly one year for my worldview to flip upside down. Prior to this, I believed that most people were good, honest, and wanted the best for others. This perspective was based on 28 years of wholesome input from church, friendly neighbors, school, basketball buddies, family, community members, and everyone else that I regularly rubbed shoulders with.

However, after I joined the department—I did what most new recruits do. I started spending more and more time with fellow officers to prove that I was 100% invested and to earn their trust.

By natural attrition, all my other relationships began to wither. I hate to admit it, but I even sacrificed my family on the altar of police loyalty. Yes, I knew I was destroying my relationship with Red. But, I didn't know that most of the time I was spending with my children was in my imagination. Somehow, I thought that because they were on my mind so much—that they would know how much I loved them. But, children need interaction and that takes time. All my time was earmarked for police.

The implications of this are simple. I stopped feeding my mind on the rich and diversified banquet of experiences from sources in the larger community. This would include the day-to-day news of sweet little girls singing in the church choir, or dedicated neighborhood youth earning college scholarships, or knuckleheaded plays by the new generation of basketball buddies or compassionate fundraisers to help the underprivileged, or the redemption of addicts who put their lives back on track.

I stopped hearing the "normal" conversation that keeps us centered, hopeful, and caring.

Instead, all my input became narrowly one-sided. This was because I was spending nearly 100% of my waking hours on the force or with police buddies. And, what do police talk about? All the trouble they see in the world.

I mean, when is the last time you called the police and said, "Can you send an officer over right away? My family just made a batch of chocolate chip cookies and we want to let the police know how much we really care about them."

Instead, every call is trouble. Someone is messing up or being messed up.

Police see people at their worst and if they are not careful, they can begin to believe the worst about people. It happens without any conscious decision.

Without knowing it, I went from "Police are here to serve the community" to "It's us (police) against them (everyone else) because they are all crazy."

I'll attempt to retrace my downward spiral from idealism (thinking the best) to cynicism (distrustful and assuming the worst).

For instance, I knew what happened in the hood. I grew up in the projects, where poverty, fatherless families, and addiction took its toll on the youth. What shocked me was when I responded to the calls in the gated communities.

These rich, white people were all jacked up too. Their kids were vandalizing property, husbands were beating their wives, mothers were addicted to prescription meds, and the dog was pooping in the neighbor's yard. After seeing both sides—the hood and the high life—I could only draw one conclusion—they were ALL messed up.

At the barbecues, we'd sit around and talk about the phone numbers we'd collected from loose women.

"This lady's got a Ph.D., a husband, three kids, and speaks two languages and she wants ME," one officer boasted.

"Yeah, well this one...I don't have to tell you... take a look...here's a photo," I said.

"Oooh wee! She hot," another officer said.

"And rich too. Her husband's never there—so I'll fix her up," I bragged. Of course, I rarely called the numbers that I collected, but they were there—feeding my ego.

Before long, our conversation would turn negative.

"Man, who would believe that all these "respectable "women are on the take?" I asked.

"Ain't none of them loyal," another added.

"Well," I said, thinking of Red, "even if they are loyal, they stop being fun. And, our wives aren't really there for us. I mean, does she really care to hear my stories at midnight when I get off work. No way. All she wants to talk about is the kids need this and the faucet needs fixed."

Yes, like most unfaithful mates, I came up with all kinds of excuses to put the blame on the innocent spouse. It could all be summed up in two sentences: Red wasn't meeting my needs. Red wasn't enough for me.

157

She wasn't enough fun. She wasn't enough woman. She wasn't. But what I failed to see was that she hadn't changed. She was still the best thing that ever happened to me. She was the loyal friend who was trying to build the bridge as fast as I was tearing it down.

I was the one who brought the cancer of selfishness into our life—the same cancer that I battled in the community every day—and whereas I saw it in other people, I could not see it in myself.

Chapter Thirty-Two

How Dare You!

One day while on patrol, I called for my partner. Life had been a bit of a whirlwind. Dispatch was quiet and I wanted to talk. So, I called my partner and he met me at the park.

We lined our squad cars up—driver's window to driver's window—and just began to unwind. We laughed, we vented, and we breathed.

A few hours later, I was called in.

"A lady made a complaint today. Said she saw you sitting two hours in the park in your car talking to another officer," my supervisor said.

"I needed to talk to my partner," I replied.

"Do it on your own time. You're paid to patrol your area—that means keep it moving. She said, 'That's what we pay taxes for.' I don't want to be getting calls like that," he added.

"Sorry, Sir. It won't happen again," I said audibly.

But silently, I was seething.

I said to myself, "How dare you! You, a woman with nothing better to do than to monitor the police—police who are out there risking their lives to keep you safe. Don't you know that we are human too. Sometimes we need to talk to our partners—someone like US who will understand! How dare you call and complain, you worthless ##*#."

Then there was the citizen that clocked me going 70 m.p.h. in my squad car. He reported that it wasn't an emergency because I didn't have my lights and siren on.

"How dare you!" I thought. "YOU are clocking an officer?"

Yes. I like to drive fast. Every once in a while I let it rip. So what. I'm a police officer. YOU—the average citizen—do not know how to treat police. Only fellow officers know how to treat an officer.

In fact, when I get pulled over by an officer—and I do—he knows exactly how to treat me.

"Good evening, Sir. Can I see your driver's license and proof of insurance?" a patrolman asked me.

"Yes, Sir," I said. I dug my license out of my wallet when he flipped on his lights. I was ready.

He took my license and studied my photo.

"Oh, so you're an officer?" he said with a sense of camaraderie. My ego was so oversized that I actually had my driver's license photo taken in my uniform. Then we'd talk about which departments we worked for and trade a couple of stories. This officer "courtesy" worked in AND out of my homestate.

He'd wrap up the conversation by telling me, "Well, watch your speed, officer."

I'd flash him my winning Officer Anthony Bryant smile and thank him very sincerely. He was in the club. I was in the club. The Officer's Club is the best club in town.

Speaking of clubs—sometimes I would drive while under the influence of alcohol. By this time, I was a pretty heavy drinker and I could hold a lot of liquor. However, I still had my limits. Sometimes, those limits were hard to distinguish—especially if I'd been drinking. Here too, officer courtesy saved me from the cost and embarrassment of getting a DUI.

Instead, the patrolling officer might ask me, "How far are you going?"

"Three more miles."

"Okay, well you probably better drive straight home. Have a good night."

This officer understood. He understood police work. He understood police culture. He understood me. Not like those bunch of morons—citizens who watched me, reported me, and obviously had no gratitude for all of my sacrifices.

Pretty soon, everyone who was not a cop was on the wanted list.

Both Sides of the Bars

Chapter Thirty-Three

Ripe for Failure

I had plenty of opportunities to break the law to enrich myself personally. One time, I rode up on a group of men who were gambling in the street. As soon as they saw my lights, they took off running. They left about $400 laying in the road. No one would have known if I had put it in my pocket, but I didn't. I played by the book.

Besides, the word was that Internal Affairs sometimes set up schemes like this to test officer honesty. Those could have been marked bills. If I took them, they'd be traced and I'd be in trouble. I doubt that I would have lost my job. More likely, I'd have to repay the money and take a couple weeks off work with no pay.

I heard about one officer that responded to a house alarm. He and his partner went in to check things out. They didn't find anything missing, so the first officer left while the second remained to do the paperwork. While he was there, he decided to take a chainsaw out of the open garage.

He might have gotten away with it, but the homeowner had a camera in the garage. A couple weeks later, the homeowner wanted to use his chainsaw, found it missing, and replayed the tape. Sure enough, he caught the officer red handed. The officer was fired.

However, as time passed—in my brief two-year career as a Chatham County Police Officer—I changed as a person. My ego grew monstrously powerful even as my ethics (corrupted by alcohol and adultery) grew significantly weaker. Add to this a cynical attitude about society—and I was headed for disaster.

163

In the last week of July 1996, my brother, Thomas Bryant, Jr.—an officer with the Savannah "City" Police Department called me. This was my big brother. The one who showed me how to survive my dad's neat-freak standards as a young boy. The one who bequeathed me the "cool shirt" and let me hang out with the seniors. The one who pulled the strings necessary so we could serve side-by-side in Germany in the Army. And, the one who inspired me to become a police officer.

This was a proud moment—standing in full uniform beside my big brother Tommy—a Savannah "City" Police Officer.

Truly, there was no one in heaven or on earth that I felt more loyal to than my big brother.

He always looked out for me and I always did what I could to help him.

"Hey, Anthony," he said. "I've got something I need to talk to you about. Can you meet me at Mayer Park tomorrow?"

I knew Tommy's voice well. Something didn't sound quite right. I wasn't sure if it was a problem with one of his girlfriends—maybe he needed me to cloak for him and say that he was at my house when he was really out tomcatting.

Or, maybe he was wanting to borrow money from his kid-brother again. Tommy always lived a flashy lifestyle and got behind on his bills. Either way, we agreed to meet the following day.

The next day, I parked my squad car next to his and joined him in his car.

"Listen," he said. "I need your help with something. There are some diamond dealers bringing up diamonds from Miami. They need an escort and they need the diamonds to be guarded in the warehouse. Then, they are going to sell the diamonds on River Street."

Now I knew that River Street in Savannah, Georgia, was a hot spot for selling all kinds of valuables or one-of-a-kind goods. In fact, last I looked, it was rated as the Number Two spot to be on Saint Patrick's day—drawing huge crowds of consumers.

But something didn't sound right. When you have been an officer for a while, you learn to trust your gut. My gut feeling was that my big brother was lying to me.

"Tommy," I said. "Give it to me straight. Tell me what's really going on."

He looked at me for a long moment. Then, he said, "Okay. It's not diamonds. It's drugs."

He saw me visibly flinch. I'd never used illegal drugs and didn't believe that anyone else should either. I was the farthest thing in the world from a drug dealer. Why was he talking to me about this?

It was almost as if he read my mind. He said, "We don't have to touch it. We don't even have to see it. The only thing we have to do is escort the cars. When we see the cars coming into town, we pull up behind the car and follow it to the warehouse. They are also going to need a guard at the warehouse, but we'll talk about that later."

I still wasn't convinced. So I just looked at him a moment.

Then I said, "I just don't like the sounds of this, Tommy."

He said, "Look man. We're not touching the drugs. We're not selling the drugs. Nobody can get you for driving behind a car!"

"Maybe it's a set up," I protested.

"Look, Anthony. I got it covered. I know the guy who's running the operation. Remember Walter Haywood? I went to school with him. Walter's cool," Tommy assured me.

"I still don't like the idea," I confessed.

"It's easy money, Anthony. It pays over $1000 for an hour of work. Think about it, man," Tommy advised.

The next day, Tommy sent me a text message, but I ignored it. However, I could not ignore the seed of greed that he'd planted in my mind. One thousand dollars in a bullet proof plan. Wow. I could really wine and dine my girlfriends. I was finding out quickly that it's hard to support a wife, two kids, and a girlfriend on the side.

The following day, he sent another text. I ignored that one too. But, I thought about the other things I could do with that money.

Back in 1996, $1000 was a lot of money. That's when Bill Clinton was President. Gosh! The cost of gas was only $1.23 a gallon. A loaf of bread cost $1.15. With $1000, I could treat Mama to a new church dress, give my brothers and sisters bigger and better birthday presents, and buy something really nice for Red and the kids. I could come out of this being a real hero!

On the third day, Tommy called me on the phone. I didn't pick up. He left a voice message. It said, "Anthony, I'm really hurting man. I need your help with this."

Both Sides of the Bars

Chapter Thirty-Four

Swallowing the Bait

I returned Tommy's call and agreed to meet with him on the fourth day. However, I had conflicting feelings and emotions. On the one hand, anything to do with drugs went against everything in my moral fiber—what was left of it.

However, this was my big brother. He always looked out for me. He needed me. He did all the homework. He said the plan was bullet proof. Tommy personally knew the guy who was in charge of the job.

The more I thought about it, the more the cynical part of the "new Anthony" began to speak up. I knew for a fact that a whole lot of drugs flowed through Savannah. There was no way that one man—one officer—could stop this problem. It had invaded the very core of society.

What difference would it really make if I drove behind a car bringing a few more drugs into the community. Those drugs were a drop in the bucket! If I didn't do it, there were a 100 other guys lined up to do it. The whole world is corrupt anyways. I might as well make the extra $1000.

On July 30, 1996, I met Walter Haywood. Little did I know that he was a convicted felon—turned CW (cooperating witness) in a FBI sting—and boy did I ever get stung!

When we met, I climbed into his car, which had been conveniently wired with cameras and microphones. He explained clearly that I would be paid to escort and guard cocaine. I gave an audible agreement that I knew what I was being asked to do.

He also explained that at all times, I needed to be in my official uniform while driving my Police car. Our entire conversation was recorded.

On August 3, 1996, I joined three other officers—my brother Tommy, Officer William Banks, and Officer Christopher Alexander (all from the Savannah Police Department)—as we escorted Walter Haywood and his fake cocaine to a rest stop on Interstate 95.

Man, I had butterflies in my stomach. I kept waiting for something to go wrong. Talk about hypervigilant. All my senses were on high alert. I was so nervous, I thought I was going to vomit. And then, it was done.

For that little service, I received a whopping $1600 cash. That was WAY more than Tommy had promised me.

Handing me that money was like handing me power.

The first thing I did was buy me some new threads. I loved to look sharp!

But, I didn't buy too many. I didn't want anyone to get suspicious.

And really, because I spread the money around, not even Red knew that I'd gotten a barrel full of cash. She was used to me having extra money. I pulled off-duty security work often, making an extra $100 or $200. I always gave her some of that too.

Then, I generously sprinkled money on my girlfriend. We ate at the best restaurant, drank the finest wine, and slept in the fanciest hotel! I gave Mama some cash as planned, gave a portion to Red, became an early Santa for the kids, and bought some early birthday presents for my brothers and sisters.

I found out that it was a bit challenging to give away $1600 in a way that it could not be accounted for. I remember that with one of my three payoffs, I helped my girlfriend fix her car. She offered to pay me back.

I said, "No. No. I don't want it back." I had to get rid of it. I felt nervous when I had that "stolen" money on me.

Five days later, I was called in for "help" again. This time, I later found out, 4.7 kilograms of real cocaine hydrochloride was used. It didn't really matter. True to their word, we never saw it or touched it. This time, we dealt with Tony. Walter told us that Tony was his right hand man, in charge of illegal drug shipments from Miami Beach, Florida. In reality, he was an undercover FBI agent.

I provided protection—in full uniform—at the warehouse for the drugs and once again provided escort service. For this added duty—security guard protection—I was paid more money. This time, I received $2500 cash.

Oh, my gosh! This was downright intoxicating. What was I going to do with so much money! Get more girlfriends? Bless my family? Live a little higher on the hog? My imagination was in a whirl.

My final involvement happened on September 20, 1996. Officer Christopher Alexander and I escorted the car carrying fake cocaine from the warehouse on Bay Street to Interstate 95. This time, my slick brother, Tommy, had talked Walter into paying him directly. Then, Tommy promised to pay the rest of his team. Later, at court, I found out that Tommy was supposed to pay me $2500, but he actually shorted me $200.

Either way, $2300 is a whole lot of money. Once again, I let it slip through my fingers—playing the hero and the high roller—and feeding my ever greedy ego.

About this time, Walter and Tony began pressuring me to recruit another officer into the program. It was the same pressure they applied to Tommy. If he wanted the money to continue—Tommy had been involved in this scam since November 1995—then he had to recruit more help. Now, I was at the same crossroads.

I didn't want to do it. It was one thing for me to make that choice to break the law. But, I really didn't want to influence another officer in a bad way. On the other hand, I REALLY liked the money. If I didn't come through with another officer, I could be cut out of the deal. So I found a fellow officer that I thought, possibly, would be interested.

When I told him the deal, he said quickly, "Nope. That's not for me."

Being a true brother—in the brotherhood of police—he did not rat me out. He just made his choice and moved on.

I thought about his response. "That's not for me." Maybe this wasn't for me either. He planted a seed. I watered it a bit.

But no. In the end, greed won out. I needed to feed this monstrous ego and it took a lot of money to give my girlfriends all the luxuries they deserved.

And then, as quickly as it started, the well ran dry. There were no more calls for escorts. I called to see if I could "be of service," but they hedged, saying that they were laying low for a while.

I was desperate. I told Walter and Tony that I had some information that they might be interested in. I had information on the Chatham County Police Department's Drug Interdiction Program. I knew the names, ranks, schedules, and methods of officers assigned to this taskforce. So on January 17 and January 23, 1997, I traded this information for $1000 cash.

Little did I know that the real reason this all dried up was because the plot was unraveling. My brother, Tommy, was fired from the Savannah Police Department on October 24, 1996—shortly after our last escort—for reasons unrelated to this sting operation.

So my brother's "team" was put out of business. In the meantime, two other teams of officers continued for a few more escorts before the whole operation was dismantled. The FBI was trying to wrap things up and have their day in court as soon as possible.

In the end—I sold my soul for a mere $7600 dollars.

It took less than a year for my wrongdoing to catch up with me. During that year, I had many sleepless nights. The three-headed monster—guilt, shame, and fear—kept invading my daydreams and dominating my nightmares.

Then, on September 10, 1997, it was over.

"Knock, knock, knock, knock, knock, knock."

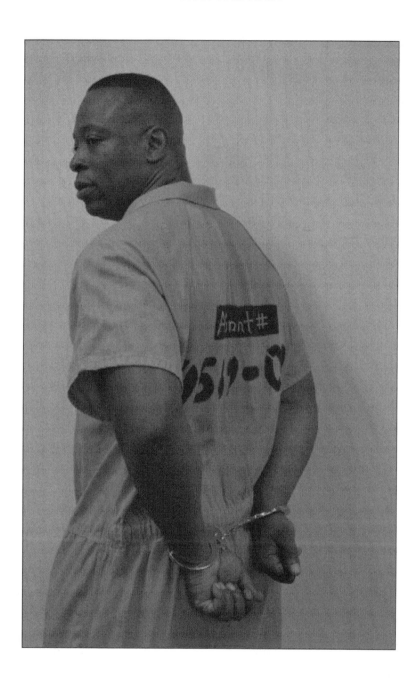

Chapter Thirty-Five

Caught on Camera

The squad car pulled up to an unmarked FBI building and the officers led me inside. They seated me in a small room with a table, a couple of chairs, a television, and the apparatus to play the video. Then, they gave me a few moments to myself.

One wall in my room had a huge interior window. I could see that I was not the only one arrested. I let my mind focus on this, rather than on my personal reality.

Before long, the lead officer came in and said, "I'm going to show you the video evidence. After you see it, you may want to plead guilty."

He started the tape. There I was, driving my police car in full uniform, escorting a "drug dealer" through Savannah. In a second video, I was talking to the undercover agent. In the final video, I was accepting cash for my involvement.

Denial disappeared instantly. I was convicted in my heart. I knew—and soon everyone would know—that I became a crooked cop.

Just then, my brother was brought down the hall. Our eyes met for a moment. He looked at me so as to say, "I'm sorry, brother. I'm sorry I got you involved in this."

I had to look away. I was angry and I focused all my anger on him. He—Tommy Bryant, Jr.—the one who always looked out for me, got me into this mess. It was his fault. In one split-second—he ruined my career, my family, and my life!

Anyone else could have asked me to do this and it would have been a flat out, "No!" But I looked up to him, I trusted him, and he used me! Tommy sacrificed his little brother to save his own skin—so he could keep his scam going.

Suddenly, Chatham County Police Chief Tom Sprague came in, riveting me back to reality. He was angry. Very, very, angry. It was the kind of anger that a man could feel when he had to answer the question: How can we trust you to keep the town crime-free when you don't even know what's going on under your own roof?

My mistake made him look bad. I made the whole Chatham County Police Department look bad because I was the only County officer arrested. The others were all City police.

So with extreme effort—he let out as much anger as he could, while yet maintaining control.

"According to....," his words blurred. Before this happened, I was actually in line for a promotion. He was supposed to be congratulating me for my new role as Community Outreach Policeman—a testament to my excellent rapport with the community and the department.

"...you are officially terminated from your employment with the Chatham County Police Department."

"Do you understand what I just read?" he asked furiously.

"Yes, Sir," I replied, with tears streaming down my face.

Then, I was left alone with my three-headed monster—shame, guilt, and fear. But this time, it wasn't invading a private daydream or nightmare. My monster was now invading my reality—a reality that was captured on video for all to see.

Chapter Thirty-Six

Bail

Eleven arrested officers were taken for mugshots. Eleven. It was the final proof that we were no longer the "good guys." Eleven officers fell for this FBI sting operation. From the looks on the other faces, we were all surprised.

Then, we were led into the court room for an immediate preliminary hearing. Judge B. Avant Edenfield heard all the accusations—attempting to aid and abet the distribution of cocaine as the primary charge—and made a decision regarding bail.

In the end, I believe that I was the only one able to post bail. (For some, it was not an option and for others it was set too high.) Due to my short involvement and excellent track record, Judge Edenfield felt that my risk of running was low.

Bail was set at $50,000. I didn't have $50,000 and neither did anyone in my family. So, imagine my indescribable relief when—of all people—my mother-in-law put up her house as collateral. That gave me hope. She believed in me. Maybe others did too.

In the meantime, we were all taken to a little known jail outside of Savannah. For the first time, we were all in one cell and allowed to talk.

It was a, "You too?" conversation. We talked about how the scam had all the right features. "You will never have to touch the drugs." "You won't have to sell the drugs." "You are ONLY providing an escort service and guard duty."

Priding ourselves in knowing the law, we quickly decided that the FBI sting was "entrapment." There WAS no actual crime. There were NO drug dealers. NO sales had taken place. Pride pushed itself back into our thinking and instead of feeling regret—we felt victimized. What right did the FBI have to run a scam on us!

Within a couple of days, we were feeling pretty hopeful. Especially, since I was granted bail—I really thought that I could beat this thing. Sure, I would lose my job—the love of my life. And, of course, I'd have to rebuild my reputation in the community. But, I would be there to raise my children—my top priority.

However, when I met with my free court appointed attorney—the guy who is paid by the city to wrap cases up as neatly and quickly as possible—he assured me the hope boat of "entrapment" was a sinking ship. Instead, he recommended that I tell the truth, plead guilty, and hope for leniency.

He didn't seem to care about me or my future. He only cared about getting his job done quickly. But in a sense, he was right. I didn't want to pay for an attorney. I later heard that one of the officers did that. He paid $50,000 and still received an 18-year prison sentence.

Also, I didn't want my case to go to trial because I didn't want all my dirty secrets spread out for world view. I knew this really happened because once a week, I was in court testifying on the domestic violence, DUIs, and other arrests that I'd made. Evidence and lifestyles exposed in these cases was sometimes shocking. My family deserved better than that.

My attorney did recommend that I be the first to plead guilty and that I snitch on the others as a way to reduce my sentence. But I knew from being a corrections officer that you never want to go into the prison system with SNITCH as your first name. And what could be more dangerous than to enter the penal system as both a cop and a snitch—with each being equally hated.

While I was waiting for the bail to process—the FBI let my mother know that she could go see her two sons in prison. That was one of the hardest days of my life.

Looking through the Plexiglas, I watched as the officer led Mama in. She tried to be strong and pick up the phone. But all she could do was cry.

There she was—a true woman of God—looking at her Anthony in jail. Anthony and Tommy—her two oldest children—who did such a wonderful job leading their siblings into adulthood. And now, the model was broken. Shattered. What happened? What went wrong?

Mama reached toward me and was stopped by the cold, inpenitrable wall of plastic. She couldn't even touch her son.

She picked up the phone and tried to say something...anything, but nothing came out. What could Mama say? What words could soothe a hurting son or her own hurting heart. Mama wept and wept.

Finally, I said, "Don't cry Mama. Please don't cry. I'm sorry. I'm really sorry."

I watched the guard lead her away. There was no doubt in my mind that Mama still loved me. She simply had nothing to give. I wept.

A few days later, I was out on bail. Red was cold—she went into survival mode. There would be no patching this thing up—even if I was acquitted.

So, I took a shower and applied for jobs online, while I waited for the children to come home. Before long, the front door opened.

"Daddy!" exclaimed Tranise when her eyes met mine. My beautiful 11-year-old daughter ran into my arms. Joy welled up in my heart so powerfully that it forced an uncontrollable flow of tears from my eyes.

"I love you so much," she said as she wiped my tears.

"I love you too, Baby," I sobbed.

Then, my four-year-old son, Anthony Bryant, Jr., came in. He was just glad to see me. He didn't know where I'd been or where I was headed. I grabbed him up—laughing and spinning. We played like nothing had ever happened.

But my daughter knew and I knew that it pained her. My face was all over the news—Big Time—CNN style. The front page of the *Savannah Morning News* screamed headlines such as: BUSTED TRUST—11 Current, Former Police Officers Indicted on Federal Drug Charges (9-11-1997).

Reporter Keith Paul began his story by saying, "They are supposed to protect us from the criminals. The 11 men –10 former or current Savannah police officers and a Chatham County officer (me)–were charged Wednesday and accused of escorting and providing protection for shipments of cocaine in and out of the area for cash."

A few lines down, he quoted Rick Pryor of the Citizens Crime Prevention.

"There is nothing lower than a corrupt politician or a corrupt police officer," Pryor said.

My Chief, Tom Sprague, was referenced as follows: "Sprague said he has 149 officers, and 'I'm proud of 148 of them.'"

Then all eleven names were listed:

Group I, Savannah police officers Keith Coleman, Frederick Gorham, Keith London, Eugene Johnson and Damion Welcome (Chatham County Sheriff's Office).

Group II, Savannah police officers Thomas Bryant Jr., William Banks and Christopher Alexander and **Anthony Bryant** (Chatham County Police Dept.)

Group III, Savannah police officers Sgt. Billy Medlock and Detective Ralph Riley.

One line was dedicated specifically to me near the end of the story. It read, "County officer Anthony Bryant was fired Wednesday after he was arrested, Sprague said."

The newspaper opened the discussion up to the public by inviting readers to call in. This fanned the flames even more.

One unnamed caller quoted in the September 12, 1997 edition of the *Savannah Morning News* said, ""This is ridiculous –you mean to tell me the only people on the police force who are crooked are African Americans? Look at New York and other cities. This is the only city where the Civil War is still going on. If you're black with any kind of authority here, it seems like you go to jail and are put on TV. This is absolutely stupid."

Pretty soon, it looked like the whole community was going to come to our aid. After all, we had clean records. Could it be that we were framed? Was this entrapment?

As the controversy continued, I focused on getting a job. I had bills to pay. Finally, I was hired as a driver for Sunbeam Bakery. They never asked, so I never told about my arrest. I delivered bread to their bakery outlets throughout Georgia from 11 p.m. to 7 a.m.

Even though I was out of jail for a few months while awaiting sentencing, my life was hard. Red didn't like me. No one trusted me. And all my police buddies abandoned me.

Wanting to normalize my life, I got the big idea to accompany Tranise on a field trip as a chaperon. I'd signed up for this prior to my arrest, but I wasn't prepared for the cold shoulder from the school and the rest of the parents.

They looked at me like, "What are YOU doing here?" They let me attend—after all, people are innocent until proven guilty—but everyone avoided me.

To be honest, the only place where I found solace was at the barbershop. One of my barbers was Reverend Hudson. As he cut my hair, he talked to me about the compassion of God. Soon, we were having weekly Bible studies. He kept it simple— discussing the basic principles of faith in Christ—so that I could gradually absorb it.

In time, I developed a thirst for more Bible truths. I visited the Overcoming Faith Church. The pastor and his wife were so Christ-like. They treated me—a man who went from cop to criminal—with the upmost respect and dignity. They reminded me that even if everything the media said was true—my life was not over yet. God could redeem me and use my life to help others. Eventually, I went through membership classes and became a member.

Fall turned into winter. Before I knew it, January 21, 1998—the day of my sentencing hearing—arrived. I made sure that I said my goodbyes—giving and receiving enough hugs and kisses to last a lifetime—because once my sentence was read, I knew that I'd be whisked away immediately.

Both Sides of the Bars

Chapter Thirty-Seven

My Day in Court

I was nervous about appearing in court. Rumor had it that Judge B. Avant Edenfield had a special hatred for drug crimes. Supposedly, he had a daughter all strung out on drugs and he'd made a personal vow to hand down 1 million years in sentencing before he retired.

I don't know if that was true or not. But when he called me up—I saw nothing but revulsion, disgust, and anger in his dark, steely eyes.

My plea was read, "At the conclusion of that proceeding (my previous day in court), the court adjudged Mr. Bryant guilty of Count 7 of the indictment charging him with an attempt to aid and abet the distribution of cocaine in violation of 21 U.S. C. 846. {Not less than 5 years and not more than 40 years imprisonment/$2,000,000 fine/At least 4 years supervised release/ $100 special assessment.}

That meant that for sure, I was going to prison for at least 5 years. My heart sank. Tranise would be 16 and little Anthony Jr. would be nine. But the Judge could give me up to 40 years. I'd be 70 years old before I got out.

I silently pleaded, "God, please have mercy on me and move the Judge to be lenient. You know that I'm turning my life around. I'm ready to do things your way. Let me be there to raise my children."

For a time, there was bantering about the amount of cocaine used in the FBI sting. It was agreed that—in all but one instance—it wasn't cocaine at all. Fake drugs were being transported. However, that really didn't matter. I'd already pled guilty. This court date was simply to receive my sentence.

After a brief review of my involvement in three scenarios, Judge Edenfield said, *"I have received a number of letters from various members of the community regarding Anthony K. Bryant, and also his record as a police officer is commendable. He received from the department or departments, and from citizens spontaneous letters commending him for his diligence while he was a police officer, assisting people, resolving difference in arguments, diffusing situations that could have gotten much worse, and by neighbors where he lived about bringing stability to the area.*

There are many, and of course, they are from people who have known him all his life, school teachers. They are attached to the presentence report and will remain a part of the permanent record."

My heart lifted. The Judge seemed genuinely moved. And, he was right. People spontaneously wrote letters in my behalf—telling the truth as they saw it. Anthony K. Bryant was not a bad man. He was a good man—with a long and positive reputation—who made a bad choice.

Of all the letters received—the one I held dearest was from the Chatham County Police Department. It was dated April 29, 1997 and titled *Citizen's Call of Appreciation.*

In part it read, *"Mr. RD said the officer came to his residence in response to a domestic situation with his daughter. The officer displayed patience, concern, and professionalism in what ended up being a civil matter. This officer reinforced Mr. RD's opinion that the majority of officers are dedicated to their profession. Mr. RD requested that if we could determine which officer assisted that the officer be given a pat on the back and a "job well done." After reviewing the calls—the Office of Internal Affairs found that Apo. A.K. Bryant (me) was the officer referred to by Mr. RD."*

I remember that call like it was yesterday. Not only did I help to diffuse a volatile situation—I genuinely cared. I made a telephone follow-up two days later to make sure Mr. RD and his family were going to be okay.

This letter was attached to my performance review by my supervisor, Lt. Smith. In part, he wrote, *"Officer Bryant strives to present himself as a role model to his peers. He is supportive of our COP program and works well with the public in problem solving. It is an honor working with Ofc. Bryant in my command."*

As I mentioned earlier, when arrested, I was actually in line for a promotion. Yes, I did something really stupid, but I did care about the public—even as I was growing more and more cynical.

The manager of the townhomes where we lived used company letterhead to write a letter directly to the Judge. She didn't just include her plea, she spoke for the whole community.

In part, Barbara A. Blythe wrote, *"WE at Cambridge Square Townhomes...It is OUR intention to ask the Court to be compassionate. WE feel that the media exposure and Mr. Bryant's loss of respect within his peer group is sufficient punishment in this case and that justice has already been served."*

And it is true. My neighbors were genuinely fond of me. I held safety meetings, raised community awareness, and reached out to the young people—all on my own time. I loved people and wanted to make our neighborhood better in the seven years that our family lived there.

There was a note from East Broad Street Elementary School thanking me for *countless hours mentoring fourth and fifth grade students*—as a volunteer. I loved and still do love helping children make good choices.

My Aunt Victoria Bryant—principal of Tompkins Middle School—wrote a letter referencing my visit to her school on Career Day. She also provided a four paragraph summary of my life, including such words as, *"Christian, prudent, respectable, confident, trustworthy, committed to his family, ability to work with people, caring, wanting to give back, and strong moral upbringing.*

She concluded by pleading in my behalf, *"If given the opportunity, I am confident that Anthony will rectify his mistakes and begin to move forward in life."*

Lastly, my good friend, who was supervisor of the Lake Mayer Recreation Park, wrote a glowing report of our 10-year friendship. Anthony Dwayne Russell said, *"I truly believe that if he had that day in 1996 to repeat over again...that the Anthony I know, the one who has made countless positive career and personal decisions in the past, would have prevailed and walked away from a situation that has altered the course of his future...his life with his wife and their two lovely children. I ask that you take into consideration Anthony's honorable past accomplishments, his family, and friends as you pass judgement for the crime that he is accused of committing."*

It was obvious—from many and diverse sources—that I, Officer Anthony Bryant, had acted *out of character*. I was not a slick, seasoned corrupt cop—the kind that the FBI was fishing for. I was an "honorable" officer who was *pressured by his big brother* to compromise.

Next, the Court heard four witnesses testify in my behalf. Red spoke first. After being questioned about our 11-year marriage, my successful military career, and my work as an officer—she pretty much stated that she would be losing her job (corporate downsizing), her husband, and her home (unable to afford it on a single income).

Then, the Court asked: What do you have to say to this Judge with regard to the sentencing that he is required to do?

Red said in part, *"I feel that it (my involvement in the escorts) was very honestly, a stupid mistake...He deserves punishment, but I ask that you be as lenient as possible. He is a loving father. Anyone can tell you that, anyone that he works with. A loving husband, always wanted the best for us. I just feel it was a very bad decision...I ask that you be as lenient as you can."*

It ripped me apart to see Red up there. I had no idea that when I became part of this "get rich quick" scheme—it would have such a dramatic domino effect in my sweetheart's life. Like me, she was losing everything. But unlike me, Red was 100% innocent.

Next up was the husband of the manager of our Townhome complex. It really touched me that these people were fighting for me tooth and nail.

He introduced himself as Urley M. Blythe, retired United States Marine Corps. He mentioned the safety seminars that I held for the residents and stated, *"He did these on his own time, at his own expense."*

He also noted generously, *"Everyone makes mistakes."* He was not given the opportunity to speak about my sentencing. He was simply dismissed.

In his place, Paul MacNeal was sworn in. Paul worked for Gulfstream Aerospace, was an associate minister at Holy Zion Holiness Church, and lived in our neighborhood. I think he talked the longest about all the good that I'd brought to the community.

Then, he was asked: What kind of a person do you think he (Anthony) is?

In part, he said, *"Good people make mistakes. I have to ask for mercy, because we are all not above reproach....Sometimes your enemies are close, but your friends and family are closer. They have influences on you. And they can lead you into things. (Referring to my big brother, Tommy.) And you just have to be careful. We make mistakes."*

Lastly, my childhood friend, Shaun Quarterman in the United States Army, showed up for me in court. Gosh! When I got so heavily involved in my police work, most of my outside friendships died from neglect. Or, at least I thought they did. But here he was, testifying in my behalf.

After establishing that Shaun had known me since 3rd grade as a close friend, neighbor, and classmate in school, he was asked, "What kind of student was Anthony?"

Shaun said proudly, *"He was always aspiring to be the best that he could be—to one day do something POSITIVE with his life and the community. We always talked about doing something positive. And THAT was what stuck with him throughout all of his life."*

He was then asked slyly, "TODAY, what do you think about Anthony Bryant?

I wondered what Shaun thought. We were squeaky clean, encouraged each other to be our best, and now I was guilty of a crime. What would he say?

Shaun said boldly, *"I respect him and love him as if he was one of my own brothers. And during the whole time that I have known Anthony, he always prided himself on being positive...and to this very day, I just feel like he made a mistake. And he is still that person who prides himself on being a positive influence for his family and his community."*

I felt a surging sense of hope. I felt that God himself had answered my prayer in that he moved so many people to write letters and to actually show up to testify in court. The Judge was given a "true picture" of who Anthony Bryant was and is. The only question was: Would the Judge allow his heart to be moved?

Finally, it was my turn to testify. I walked the court through my track record, beginning with my marriage, followed by six years of honorable service in the Army during Operation Desert Shield and Operation Desert Storm. I talked about my mentoring and volunteer work in the schools, and my work with the Sheriff's Department and finally the Chatham County Police Department.

Then, in part, I said, *"Sir, I did make a mistake. I'm not a bad individual. I'm very sorry. I beg for leniency, Sir. Because that (breaking the law) is not common place with me. I ask that you please take how I have conducted myself throughout my 30 years of life and I ask you for leniency, Sir. I am not a bad person. I made one bad decision that will haunt me for the rest of my life. I do apologize."*

Judge B. Evant Edenfield let me and everyone else in Court know that he genuinely heard all the fine testimony. He said, in part, *"It is commendable. You have done some fine things. You were held in high esteem by members of the forces, both Armed Forces and other police agencies."*

Then he changed channels and added, *"Yet, we have this HORRIBLE BREACH OF TRUST."*

He acknowledged my brother's influence, saying, *"I do not doubt for a moment that you were directed by a kinsman, your brother. However, you would be the first to admit, you were GROWN and KNEW that the responsibility of a police officer was possibly even higher than that of a non-police officer, a citizen."*

Then, he switched his focus back to my 30 years of good deeds—minus my six months of compromise—and said, *"The testimony of all those who have known you and met you and their presence here today ATTESTS TO THE GOODNESS YOU HAVE DONE."*

I really felt that Judge Edenfield drew the distinction between me and a few of the other officers that were caught. Some of officers had been bending the rules for many years. In fact, that is why the FBI set up the sting. For years, citizens had complained about the corruption in the Savannah CITY Police Department.

Even the breaking story in the *Savannah Morning News* said, "...the Crime Commission—a citizen crime watchdog group—has called for an investigation of the *city* police department **since 1992."**

Unfortunately, instead of purging the city of 11 longstanding corrupt cops—most of the officers arrested were clean cut guys who *acted out of character* in a fake drug scenario. The problem was—they were being treated like long-time criminal cops—as I was soon to find out.

Judge Edenfield then announced, ***"Pursuant to the Sentencing Reform Act of 1984, it is the judgement of the***

Court that Anthony Bryant is committed to the custody of the Bureau of Prisons for the term of 148 months."

Even though the Judge kept talking, my ears stopped hearing. My heart sank. 148 months. That is 12 years and 4 months. That is a lifetime sentence for a 30-year-old man with children. Suddenly, I felt weak all over. It was all that I could do to keep myself from passing out.

The last thing I heard was, "You are remanded to the custody of the Marshal. Hearing concluded."

Without even a moment to say goodbye to Red or to hug my Mama, I was escorted out of the courtroom. One hundred and forty-eight months of prison fell into my future—pulverizing every plan and prospect that I'd ever dared to imagine. It was all gone—after one day in court.

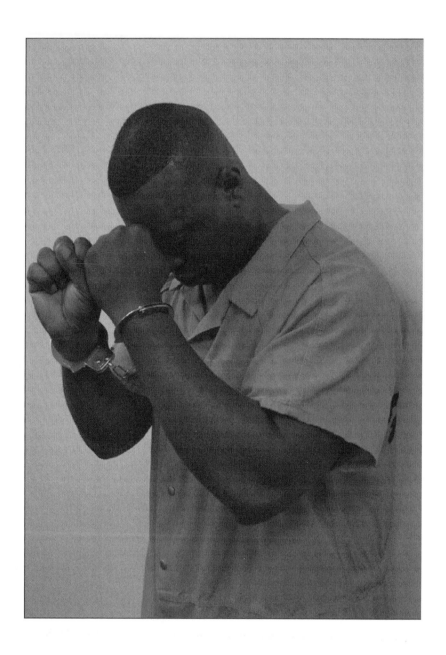

Chapter Thirty-Eight

The Holding Tank

When I arrived at the United States Penitentiary, Atlanta (Georgia), I was ordered to strip off my jumpsuit. In its place, I was issued an old, stained, whitish colored T-shirt, along with a pair of beige elastic-waist cotton pants. This set the expectation for the "punishment" I would receive as a "dirty cop."

Next, I was placed in isolation for 30 days. This might seem like torture, and it was. But it was better than being fed alive to my home state inmates—who'd all been fed my story from local media.

The "Atlanta Pen" had a reputation of being one of the worst in the country. As corrections officers, we used to talk about it. It was the one place that we all agreed we would never work at. Never. It was too violent. No pay would make it worth the risk.

So here I was in the Atlanta Pen. I figured that this was the FBI and local law enforcements way of making an example out of us.

I could just hear the other officers across the state and maybe the nation saying, "Did you hear where they sent those 11 cops who were busted by the FBI?"

"Yeah. The Atlanta Pen. Man, it will be a miracle if they make it out of there alive."

However—like waterboarding—those in power knew exactly how to walk the fine line of making our prison time as painful as possible, while yet allowing us to survive.

So, the first 30 days, I was put in complete isolation. That meant that I was only let out of my 5' x 7' cell for an hour a day. There was a small, enclosed area where I could walk and/or exercise alone. Also, about every other day, I had the opportunity to take a shower.

My whole world came to a stop. This was for real. I would not see my family for 10 years. What kind of a role model had I been? Why did I listen to my brother? Left in this vacuum—I began to beat myself down into a pit of hopelessness and despair.

Two days into my stay, I asked for a Bible—but with no one to explain it and no one to share it with, the pages felt empty. Also, there was a book cart. The guards brought it around when they felt like it. I read some great books—one author I especially remember was John Grisham. The stories temporarily transported me to another place and time. But when I turned the final page, I had to face my cell and my self.

The guards also gave me a deck of playing cards. I played solitaire. But mostly, I shuffled the cards and used them as a guide for my exercise. If I pulled out a five—I did five military push ups. If I pulled out a Jack—I did 10 sit ups, and so on. I wanted to be iron tough by the time I walked into the prison that I would be eventually assigned to.

Still—it was psychological torture. To have fallen from grace and have no one in the world to talk to was horrible. So, I also spent a lot of time praying. I prayed for God to forgive me, but I also prayed for God to give me some relief.

What came next, bent my soul in the opposite direction. After 30 days of solitary confinement—suddenly three other inmates were assigned to my 5' x 7' cell. That meant four guys were locked into this tiny space for 23 hours a day.

Since I had seniority, I claimed the top bunk. It was as far away from the in-room toilet as possible. One inmate slept on a bunk under me, and a second inmate on a bunk under him. The last guy had to sleep on the floor on a mat.

So how do four guys survive in a 35 square-foot cell for 60 days? We made rules. Basically it was common sense.

1) Don't Touch. Don't touch me or anything that belongs to me. I don't have much and so I'm very protective of anything I have left. That includes: Don't ever sit on my bunk without being invited.

2) Respect. Think before you speak. Use manners. Be considerate. When it's time to sleep, keep quiet.

3) Privacy. When someone is on the toilet, turn your face to the wall.

The hardest thing to deal with was the "open air" toilet. This commode had a high pressure water system. So when it was flushed, water and debris could spray in the room. That is why I chose the top bunk.

Also, imagine four guys eating prison food while under extreme emotional duress. I can't think of a better recipe for intestinal upset. So, it seemed like someone was always on the toilet or passing gas. It was—in effect—like living in a giant toilet.

Both Sides of the Bars

Thirty-Nine

Grace Period

One day in April of 1998, the guards removed me from my cell. I was placed in a transport van and taken to Federal Medical Center—a federal prison in Lexington, Kentucky. Finally, I would be allowed to build some semblance of a life as a member of the prison population. I could get a job, volunteer, work out in the gym, do crafts, take classes, make friends, create a wholesome routine to pass my 10-12 years.

But that would come later. My first task at hand was to enter the population as easily and as carefully as possible. I'd watched newcomers do this for three years when I was a corrections officer in Chatham County. I knew that how an inmate walks in on the first day has a HUGE bearing on how the rest of his stay will be.

The key is to walk in confident, but not cocky.

1) **Confident**: Standing up tall and strong. I'm here to serve my time and I mind my own business. I know how to take care of myself.

2) **Cocky**: I don't belong here. I'm better than other people. {An arrogant newcomer is just asking for someone to take them down a peg. A cocky newcomer is seen as an insult and a challenge to the inmate population.}

3) **Cotton Candy**: Crying, showing signs of fear, cowering, and flinching. These newcomers are seen as being as soft as cotton candy and ready to be kissed on.

Even if you do everything right on the parade into the prison—it isn't over yet. The next question you have to answer is: Who are you? Are you a thug—interested in contraband, drugs, bootleg alcohol, and gambling? Do you line up with the blacks, the whites, the Hispanics or another ethnic group? Are you one of the Georgia boys—021? The last three digits of your inmate number tell what state you are from. Are you going to be loyal to the guys from your state?

In most prisons, you are given a seven to 14 days grace period. It's an unspoken "hands off" courtesy. It's kind of like the NFL picks—which team will you end up on. But it's also very different. Some people are looking to recruit you for their team. Other inmates are predators and want to "feed you" to their teammates.

The problem with picking a "team" is that, while the team will protect you, you will be required to fight for the team when another team challenges it. So, I made the choice to refuse membership to any team.

The only team that I joined was the Christian team. That probably saved me, because I'm a little guy. At the time, I was 30 years old. I weighed 135 pounds and stood 5' 7". But in prison, believe it or not, if an inmate is true to his faith, other inmates will respect that.

The question is: Am I a true Christian? Inmates have no patience for pretenders. They don't require you to be perfect, but if you are swearing like a sailor, lying, stealing, or cheating—you are a liar! You are not a Christian and you are open game.

A real Christian is an inmate who looks out for other inmates interests, helps others in need, is self-sacrificing, kind, considerate to all, has the highest respect for others, and truly treats fellow inmates in the way that he wants to be treated.

The thing about prison is this—there is no escape. There is no harder place to be a pretender than in prison. Eyes are on you 24/7. People are watching you eat, sleep, exercise, pray, shower, work, and play. There is no place to hide. There is no room for a double-life.

Both Sides of the Bars

Forty

Who is the Leader?

Even though the inmate population accepted me as a true Christian—I still had to navigate about 2000 men. The key was to figure out who was the leader of each group. Then, I needed to assure each leader that I was not a threat to their team.

It only took about four days to identify the leaders. With a bit of close observation, I could readily see who was kissing up to who and who was serving who. The hard part was to make an introduction. I looked for a natural way to meet them.

I met one leader on the basketball court. I've always been pretty good with the ball—which naturally earned me respect on the court. My goal was to interact with the leader in such a way that he would conclude and tell his group, "Anthony is okay. Let him be."

It wasn't so easy with the leader of the Hispanics. He was clearly unapproachable. It would have been a huge mistake to attempt contact. Instead, I watched his co-captains and secondary leaders. One guy had a great sense of humor. We forged a connection.

It really paid off when I was in the commissary (the only place where inmates are allowed to buy food or supplies while in prison). When it was my turn, I bought the last 3-pack sleeve of tuna. Then, the Hispanic inmate placed his order.

I heard him say, "No more tuna. Man, I really need that."

I said, "I've got a three pack. You can have one of mine."

He looked at me. In prison, nothing is ever free. Young, green inmates don't know this and they are selling their souls by accepting free honeybuns or chips from older inmates who want to be their "friends."

He offered to pay me.

I said, "No problem. Down the line, I may need a can and you can give it to me then. We're cool."

He looked at me, smiled as if to say "you're okay" and then gave me a handshake. Later, I found out that the can was not for him. It was for his leader. He told his leader what I did and that scored points for me. In my kindness, I proved that I cared about Hispanics. I wasn't just looking out for myself or my "kind." The leader let his team know, "Anthony is okay. Hands off."

One of the hardest leaders to meet was the head of the Muslim group. Like the Hispanic leader, I had to look for a natural opportunity to help him, because it would be seen as arrogant to approach him without an invitation. At the same time, it was dangerous to navigate the prison system without his "blessing."

Over time, I noticed that he enjoyed working in the craft room. Now I personally loathed arts and crafts—but my life was on the line. So, I took an interest in his interest. Of all the crafts, he made beautiful purses which he then sent outside the prison as gifts to his family or for resale.

The next time I was at the commissary, I bought some beautiful silky material. Then, I went into the craft shop. The first time I did this, I was completely ignored. However, I stayed there and attempted to work with my fabric.

The next time I went in—while he was in there—he ran out of the fabric he needed to line a purse. It just so happened that it was exactly the fabric that I had bought. Also, the commissary was at least temporarily out of this stock.

First, he asked another guy in the room, "Do you have any more of this fabric?"

"No," came the reply.

"I do," I said lightly.

He looked at me as if to ask, "Who are you?" and then said, "Okay."

He took my fabric and it was a rapport building moment. From then on, I took little opportunities to make eye contact or small observations—stitching together a fragile relationship one thread at a time.

Over time, I walked this tightrope of relationships successfully. I proved that I was not part of any clicks or teams, while simultaneously refraining from insulting or offending the many cultures within the system.

Both Sides of the Bars

Forty-One

Know Your Place

The most volatile place in the prison is the dayroom. It may look like open seating—but the surest way to get beat up is to take a seat in the front by the television. Front row seats are reserved for the leaders.

Knowing this, I chose to sit in the back of the dayroom. Overtime, as I got to know people, they would invite me to sit by them. Gradually, I worked my way up to where I could sit in almost any seat in the room—except the front row!

I also knew my place in the pecking order of crimes. The worst thing you can be is a child molester or someone who beat up an elderly person. Even hardened inmates have their standards and they have no tolerance for people who prey upon those who cannot protect themselves.

Next to this is a crooked cop. If a cop is in prison, he's a crooked cop. He was supposed to be keeping the community safe, serving the needs of others, and defending the defenseless. A crooked cop was using the inside track of trust for personal gain. This was unforgivable.

So, for me, rule #1 was: Never tell anyone I was a cop. Instead, I talked about my charges. I was arrested for attempt to aid and abet the distribution of cocaine. So, in short, like so many others in prison, I was in for drug charges. Drug charges are considered pretty benign. No one in prison hates you for that.

Interestingly, in "real life" people often ask: What do you do for work? However, in prison, this is rarely the question. They only ask: What are you in for? When do you get out?

Both Sides of the Bars

Forty-Two

Attempted Suicide

In life—both inside and outside of prison—we have a public image and an inner private self. When I stepped into the federal prison in Lexington, Kentucky, I managed my public image extremely well. But I couldn't escape my inner self.

As I continued to struggle with the reality of losing my wife—who was no longer accepting my phone calls—and the prospect of my children growing up without their dad, it was just too much to bear.

I silently battled with guilt, shame, and chronic depression—pushing me to the point of wanting to end my life. When I thought about it, the last thing that I wanted was for my children to visit their dad in prison. So, suicide seemed to be the best option for me.

For weeks, I collected aspirins and various medications from different inmates who went to the infirmary.

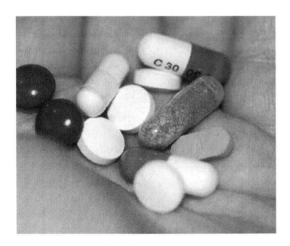

My plan was to accumulate enough medications, so that when I swallowed the entire cocktail —I would die peacefully in my sleep.

I remember sitting on the edge of my bed with the pills in one hand and a cup of water in the other. I was crying uncontrollably, but felt that this was the only way to end the stigma, the pain, and the embarrassment that I had caused to myself and my family.

As I was getting ready to end it all, I heard a voice (not audible) urging me to look under my mattress. This was really strange because I'd never had a reason to look under there.

I ignored the voice in my head—chalking it up to extreme stress. However, as I attempted to take the pills, the voice in my head yelled louder: LOOK UNDER THE MATTRESS!

At this point, I decided to obey.

When I pulled the mattress back, there was a hardcover Gideon bible.

I picked it up.

Though I'd been raised in church from infancy through adulthood, I realized that I didn't know anything about this book—except that it was sacred. It was a book to be treated with respect.

Slowly, I began to turn the pages. I didn't know what I was looking for, but was immediately drawn to Ecclesiastes 7:8 which reads, "Better is the end of a thing than its beginning, and the patient in spirit is better than the proud in spirit."

I had no earthly idea what this verse meant or how it applied to me. So, I remained intent on my original plan—to end my life. However, the nagging voice now told me: Visit the prison chapel.

I was not in the mood to visit any chapel, church, priest, or rabbi, for that matter. All I wanted to do was end my life, once and for all.

I wrestled with my choices. After much reluctance, I went to the prison chapel. Oddly enough, it was completely empty. Usually, with an inmate population of nearly 2,000—someone is in there. But, not this time.

As I walked inside, I saw a large radio and an old brown piano with a case on top. When I opened the case, I found dozens of gospels on cassette tapes. I never listened to gospel music in the past, but under the circumstances, I decided to rummage around in the box.

The only artist I recognized was Kirk Franklin. I knew his song, *Stomp*." My friends and I used to dance to it—but it wasn't praise dancing we were doing! However, when I thought back on the lyrics, maybe it was gospel.

In part, the lyrics say:

Lately, I've been going through some things that
really got me down
I need someone, somebody to help me, come and
turn my life around
I can't explain, I can't obtain it, Jesus your love
is so, it's so amazing
It gets me high up to the sky and when I think
about Your goodness

It makes me wanna stomp, makes me clap my
hands
Makes me wanna dance and stomp
My brother can't you see I got the victory?
Stomp!

The more I looked at that cassette, the more it felt like I was looking at an old friend. I took the cassette out of the case, walked it over to the cassette player and popped it in. However, when I pressed the play button, what came out was not *Stomp*.

Instead, I heard Kirk Franklin's song, *My Life is in Your Hands*. As those words bathed my hurting soul, I was instantly and forever transformed.

You don't have to worry
And don't you be afraid
Joy comes in the morning
Troubles they don't last always
For there's a friend in Jesus
Who will wipe your tears away
And if your heart is broken
Just lift your hands and say

Oh, I know that I can make it
I know that I can stand
No matter what may come my way
My life is in your hands

At the conclusion of the song, there was no doubt in my mind that God was speaking to me. Although I did not understand the meaning of the scriptures, God knew that I loved music. I was able to connect His meaning and purpose for my life through the avenue of music.

I fell to my knees in total submission—crying like a baby. For the first time, I felt a peace and calm about my incarceration. It was a peace that I had never felt before.

No longer did I feel the need to end my life. This was God's way of letting me know through the bible verse, Ecclesiates 7:8, that the ending of this prison sentence would be better than the beginning.

I just had to hold on, because my life was now in His hands. The comforting words in that song gave me the strength and confidence needed to persevere through the highs and lows of prison life. I now had a focus. I was ready to see what God had in store for me during my years of imprisonment.

Both Sides of the Bars

Forty-Three

Let the Sun Shine

With my pride, power, and prestige stripped away—I was now free to serve others. As a start, I volunteered as the chaplain's assistant. One of my duties was to distribute care packages—with soaps, toothbrushes, and snacks—to help new inmates until their commissary accounts were established. With each care package, I offered genuine encouragement.

I met with inmates who were leaders from all the religions and ordered supplies for their religious services. If they needed candles or anything else—they ordered through me. It brought me great joy to see their needs met. It also put me in association with a growing number of people of faith.

Additionally, I kept feeding myself spiritually by consuming inspirational messages from three spiritual leaders in particular. T. D. Jakes, Sr., bishop of The Potter's House especially moved me by his book, *He-Motions*, and his music, such as his award-winning album *A Wing and a Prayer*. I connected so tightly with Dr. Tony Evans' words—that I felt as though he was walking me through my daily journey. He said his goal was to "transform lives" and that is exactly what he did for me. Our prison had some of his videos in our library and his book, *No More Excuses: Be the Man God Made You to Be,* was exactly what I needed to hear. Also, I tuned in to his program on my radio often.

I also found Eva Marsee one day when I was depressed and scanning through the radio stations. I stopped my search, when I heard her preaching on divorce. How timely. I was laying on my bunk—totally depressed—holding my divorce papers in my hand. Her radio show, *Stir the Fire,* did what it was intended to do. It got me up and out of my misery and on to helping others. I actually wrote her a letter of thanks and we corresponded throughout my incarceration and beyond.

Next, I applied for a job with UNICOR—Federal Prison Industries. Amazingly, due to my extensive background in Army communications—I was awarded a position in the procurement billing department. That meant I was talking to real businesses in the outside world via the telephone and computer, checking on their orders of office furniture that was crafted right in the prison.

If I'd been a free man, the job would have paid about $2500 per month. Because I was in prison, it only paid me $120 a month. But the value to my life was priceless. This job gave me back my dignity and buoyed my self-esteem.

With those two anchors in place—meeting my spiritual and my secular needs—my gloom lifted and the sun really began to shine in my life.

By November of that year, my two children, Tranise, age 12, and Anthony Jr., age 5, visited me in Lexington.

What they found was a role model dad who had something to give.

I was on the path to a better life.

My sister, Tanika, loyally stood by me—coming to visit as often as she could.

She also sent me a monthly allowance— which makes all the difference in the world for an inmate surviving prison.

Also, my sister, Tanika, supported me with visits when possible and provided a regular allowance. On average, she sent $60 every month.

For an inmate, that means so much. It meant the difference between ill-fitting prison-issued shoes and Nike, New Balance, or Adidas footwear. It meant the difference between bland cafeteria food—and the ability to purchase fresh fruit, canned meats, and tasty snacks. Mostly, it meant the difference between isolation and the ability to contact my loved ones by means of telephone calls, gifts, and letters.

I had been given so much—a second chance—that I was searching for ways to give to others. For the first time since childhood, my motives were pure. I wanted to do what was right for God and for my neighbors—where ever I happened to be.

Both Sides of the Bars

Forty-Four

Do the Hustle

Soon, I settled into my new life. This life—life in prison—was preparing me for my new life when I was released. I stopped looking backwards so much. I stopped thinking about the 10 Christmas's that I would miss with my family. I kept focused on my ultimate goal—to let God mold me into the man I could be.

Instead of looking at the limitations of prison—I looked for opportunities. I asked the question: What CAN I do? Pretty soon, I found my hustle. A hustle is a skill, talent, or ability that other inmates are willing to pay for. It adds to your pocket change, but it also adds to your identity and self-worth.

One of my first hustles was nachos. On Friday nights, I'd find five or six empty bowls on my bed with an order that needed to be filled before the weekly movie began. For three dollars—I'd fix simple nachos and cheese. We never use cash in prison—so the fellas would pay me with postage stamps. Three dollars equals six postage stamps.

I offered a variety of nachos for various prices. The meat lovers nachos was the most expensive—seven dollars—and included three or four types of summer sausage and canned meats.

Recipe for:

Anthony 's Prison Nachos

Ingredients:
Doritos or plain Tortilla Chips
Meat (summer sausage, can chicken or tuna, from commissary).
Vegetables (from commissary or black market from the inmate kitchen workers). Chili
Honey
Cheese
Seasonings

Directions:
1. Slice all your vegetables and meat and place them in a bowl together.
2. Add your seasonings (salt, pepper, etc...) to the bowl of meat and veggies
3. Microwave for approximately three minutes. On each minute you would stir clockwise seven circular movements.
4. Place one layer of chips on a plate or in a bowl.
5. Melt cheese
6. Place meat and veggies on bottom layer of chips
7. Add cheese
8. Repeat layering process (chips, meat, veggies, then cheese) until finished.
9. You can top it off with honey to give it a honey roasted flavor

In turn, I counted on other inmates for their hustles. My weekly haircut—bald fade—cost $5. About twice a month I paid $5 for a guy to iron a hard crease into my uniform. And occasionally, I treated myself to a delicious fruit salad that cost $4-6. Why did I buy these things? It made me feel good. It felt good to take care of myself, look sharp, and keep my standards high. And I liked the power of choice—even if they were "small" choices.

Despite the fact that life was going well for me in Lexington, I kept pushing to be transferred to Jesup Federal Prison Camp in Jesup, Georgia. I really missed my family and wanted to be closer to my kids.

The chaplain and other people who cared about me discouraged me from transfering. They told me that my crime was still too fresh. Being close to home in a high profile crime was an invitation for mistreatment. They begged me to stay, but I didn't listen. So in June 2000, I was finally transferred to Jesup.

My friends were right. Going to Jesup was a huge mistake. The inmates knew that I was a cop and they made it tough on me. During my stay, someone planted marijuana in my cell and accused me of having possession of illegal drugs. I was drug tested several times—each time testing negative—but the unfounded charges raised my security level. Within three months, I was shipped out to the Federal Correctional Institution in Yazoo, Mississippi. Though it was a hard way to get there, Yazoo proved to be one of my favorite stops in my prison journey.

First, I met Tony Park—a Tallahassee Florida State Trooper—imprisoned for selling drugs from his patrol car. Like me, he'd become a true man of faith. However, he was farther along the path and was a great help in strengthening my beliefs.

Tony had such a fine reputation that he was known by the guards and inmates alike as the "inmate preacher"—a man who could be trusted.

At the same time, I landed an awesome job in the recreation department—complete with my own office, computer, and extensive latitude in the development of the recreational calendar for the prison. I mention all of this to lead up to the new hustles that I discovered at Yazoo.

222

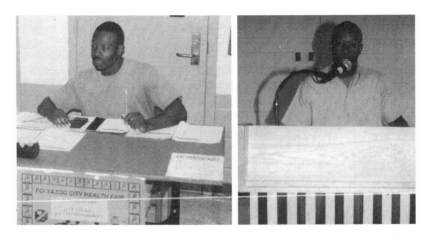

I became a positive force at Yazoo. I ran a health fair and preached about the power of God to transform lives.

Interview Etiquette

This was a popular class that I taught. It was based on Benjamin Franklin's premise: If you fail to plan, you are planning to fail. This class provided a plan for upcoming job interviews upon release from prison. I encouraged inmates with many years of incarceration before them to take the class, so they could keep living for their release date.

One commonly asked question: How do I mark the box, "Have you ever been incarcerated?"

My answer: Write the words, "Please allow me to explain." Then, realize that nearly everyone in the U.S. has a family member, friend, or someone they know of who has been in prison.

So, how do you "explain?" I would tell the class, research says that you should tell the prospective employer why you were imprisoned and then focus on what you LEARNED.

As an example, I would tell the class—I was imprisoned for attempt to aid and abet in the sale of cocaine. What does that mean? I never saw drugs, used drugs, or sold drugs. Instead, I took an opportunity and looked the other way when this was happening.

What did I learn? There is no amount of money and no degree of family loyalty that could ever get me to go against my God-given values again.

I also shared with the class the need to clarify their charge. One man was arrested and confined to prison for kidnapping. What did he do? He and his girlfriend were arguing in his parked car. She was angry and didn't want to listen to his side of the story. So he popped the door locks and wouldn't let her out until he had his say.

It just so happened that a policeman drove by, saw the ruckus, and questioned them. The girlfriend accused the guy of not letting her leave (keeping her against her will) and he ended up in prison. My point: Always explain your charge and then tell what you LEARNED.

In one of my classes, an inmate asked, "What should I say if I've been in prison more than once?"

I said, "Tell them the truth. Tell them you are a slow learner. You've had to bang your head on the wall a few times before you finally got the message that you needed to change your life. But now you know that you want a better a life for you and your family."

We also talked about how to greet a future employer. We practiced our firm handshake, while smiling and looking the person in the eyes. Of course, a handshake with a woman should be a little more gentle—but not limp.

We talked about posture, word choice, enthusiasm, and follow up. Usually, I had 20-30 inmates in my class. Each of them paid $5 per session. It was a good hustle for me and a good value for them. But mostly—it paid by feeding my soul. I knew that I was adding value to their world. We kept it practical. We kept it light. And, we kept it fun.

Tutoring

I tutored in many subjects. The most popular included GED prep, resume building, and public speaking. The idea is this: Teach what you know. Teach what you are passionate about. In hindsight, I think that many inmates took my classes through the side door. They didn't directly care about public speaking. However, they knew that for the 30 or 60 minutes that they were in my class, they were going to be surrounded by other guys who were looking forward, thinking positively, and laughing while learning.

Ab Class

Most inmates don't know this, but the recreation department is very open to suggestions from the inmate population for physical fitness classes. They are even more inviting if the inmate comes with a plan.

Now for me, the muscles on my body that seemed most inclined to shine were my abdominals. In fact, it was at Yazoo that I was given the nickname "Six-Pack." Soon, guys were asking me how THEY could have a six pack like mine.

So, I went to my supervisor with a plan.

I told him, "I'd like to put together an Ab class. It will add diversity to our program and because exercise reduces stress and less stress means less fights—it will be good for our prison.

He smiled and said, "Sounds good. What do you need from me?"

I said, "We'll need to buy 15 exercise balls and 15 ab wheels. Oh, and I'll need to print up some flyers. It's going to be a tough class, but we'll get results. I already have a class schedule."

It was done! Then, a fun thing happened. The supervisors would pop in and watch us work out. Clearly, we were putting our hearts and souls into our goals. One of the supervisors caught wind that we were having an in-house contest at the end of the class to see who had the best six pack.

This supervisor knew some professional bodybuilders in the "real" world. He invited them to come in and judge our competition. So, we actually had a Muscle Mania Body Pose Contest—inviting any inmate to join in.

On September 17, 2004, we oiled up and put on shorts. Hundreds of inmates sat in the audience. The professionals made their choices. In the end, I came in 2nd Place. While my six-pack was the best, my skinny legs just couldn't stand up to the 1st Place muscled man in my division.

But, it was a proud moment. The entire event became a blessing for the whole prison because we worked together— inmates and supervisors—and built momentum that caught the attention of the outside world.

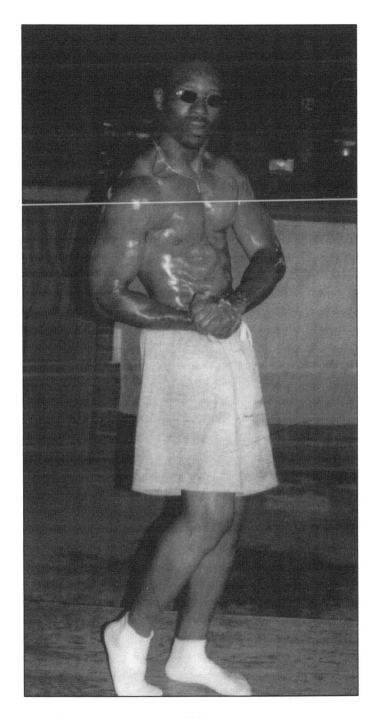

Prison Hustles

Bad Hustles

1.) Selling drugs, alcohol, or other illegal items not allowed in prison.
2.) Making tattoos.
3.) Extortion
4.) Gambling
5.) Snitching (Setting up officers to engage in illegal activities and then telling on them in hopes of getting a reduced prison sentence.)

Good Hustles

1.) Braid hair
2.) Wash clothes
3.) Iron clothes
4.) Cook food (Nachos, Fruit Salad, Burritos)
5.) Tutor
6.) Cut hair
7.) Teach an educational or fitness class
8.) Make leather belts, purses, or items in the hobby craft workshop

Forty-Five

Home Stretch

That mountain top experience of Muscle Mania came right on the heels of my 37th birthday. I realized that my race was more than halfway over. If I continued on my course, I'd be released in about three-and-a-half years. Now that's a time frame a man can live with.

Though I'd be bounced around a few more times, shipping out to Seymour Johnson Air Force Base Federal Prison Camp in Goldsboro, North Carolina the very next month, and then two years later to my final destination at Williamsburg Federal Correctional Institute in Salters, South Carolina—I now knew how to survive and even thrive in prison.

Visits from my children—being able to show them that I was all right and seeing for myself that they were okay—made it so much easier for me to look to the future with hope.

It's a different world, but I encouraged everyone I could to head straight to the chaplain upon arrival in a new prison. There, they would find people like me, who could tell them who to trust and how to navigate the neighborhood. And, they could take the opportunity to get their lives right with God and right with themselves.

I was quick to tell new inmates, "Don't let them lock you up twice. They've got your body. Don't let them lock up your mind."

I'd also explain the difference between good time and bad time. I'd say, "Good time is educating yourself so you can have a better life when you are released. Good time is thinking ahead, planning, and making the best of your situation. Good time is keeping focused on your second chance. That's the chance you get when you are released."

Then, I'd explain bad time by saying, "Bad time is getting involved in the wrong crowd. That can lead to violence, isolation, and more time. Bad time is giving up on yourself, letting yourself become a victim, instead of a victor. Bad time is a choice YOU make."

Now I don't want to sugarcoat the prison experience. I saw a lot of horrific things when I was behind the bars— stabbings, rapes, fights, suicide attempts, illicit drugs and alcohol, gambling, and rampant homosexuality.

Just speaking to the last point, in my estimation, in a medium security prison with about 2000 inmates—it seemed that about 25% were openly homosexual, 40% were closet homosexuals, and 35% were straight. What I mean by a closet homosexual is that they act straight, but you might catch them kissing another guy or willingly engaging in sex. Then, on visitation day, you'd see him kissing his wife with the same mouth that he'd used to kiss a guy.

Many inmates call homosexual acts "doing time" or "survival"—meaning that since abstinence is not an option for them, they work with what is available. Most homosexual sex is consensual, but there are thugs. For thugs, sex is not so much about pleasure—it is more about overpowering and degrading others. Either way—the real world has it rumored that staying sexually intact in prison is a real challenge—and it is true.

For me, I made the choice to stay straight and wait. I believed that this was what God wanted for me. Also, a note on fights. It would be virtually impossible to get out of prison without ever being involved in an altercation. That is why it's important to stay as physically fit as possible, show respect for everyone and watch your associations. Also, stay out of places like restrooms in the wee hours of the night where you might see something you don't want to see. People will beat you up if they believe you witnessed something.

Again, aside from restoring my relationship with God and letting him mold my life, one of the best moves I made in prison was to refuse to align with any single group—other than the Christians. So, when the whites and blacks had issues or the Mississippi boys offended the Georgia boys—I was on neutral ground with all of them. I was simply a man of God and good to all.

10 Commandments of Prison Survival

1. **Don't be a snitch.** Child molesters and snitches are the two most hated people in prison. It is best to "look away" before anyone sees you see anything illegal or illicit.
2. **Do not discuss your crime.** Some inmates collect information and use it against you by testifying in court in hopes of reducing their sentence. Never discuss sexual crimes.
3. **Do not gamble.** There are no winners and you could end up dead. If you lose—you can't afford to pay and if you win and make the wrong person angry you are doomed.
4. **You MUST work out.** Working out reduces stress, passes the time, and strengthens you mentally and physically. You have to be ready to defend yourself.
5. **Avoid conflict with fellow inmates.** Avoid getting involved in drama. Don't get provoked to fight—it starts a cycle. A non-win situation for you.
6. **Stay away from gangs.** Gangs and cliques have rivals. It is best to avoid the temptation or pressure to join. Instead, be respectful of everyone.
7. **Get connected with your faith group.** Prisons support virtually every faith. Find your faith group to associate with so you can find peace and comfort with people you trust.
8. **Start planning on Day 1 for your release.** Proper planning prevents poor performance. Do research and

plan for your job, place to live, budget, and the rest. Get family or friends on the outside to help you.

9. **Stay away from homosexuals.** Prison is lonely and without sex the time is more difficult. Homosexuals prey on the weaknesses of those wanting sex and will provide it in an instant.

10. **Communicate with loved ones and friends often.** Maintaining contact with family and friends will keep you looking forward. It will also give you a sense of normalcy.

Both Sides of the Bars

Forty-Six

Going Home

May 15, 2008, my sister, Tanika, drove up to the prison gates. As I walked toward her, cheers, applause, and well-wishes pounded in my ears from inmates of all sizes, shapes, and colors. Tears welled up in my eyes as I realized that I'd met some really cool guys in prison and I was actually going to miss them.

More tears came as I stepped outside the final gate—a free man and a better man. I actually viewed my years in prison as a spiritual retreat. God transformed me in those 10 years and four months.

I actually believe that God had to strip me of all the things that I thought made me a man—prestigous career, big house and fast car, wholesome family, and loyal friends—so that my experience of isolation and separation would let me see the one thing I was really missing in my life. Jesus Christ.

It did me good to wear #09589-021—until I earned the right to accept my name Anthony K. Bryant. Before going behind bars, my name gradually came to mean arrogant, self-serving, and power-hungry. During my incarceration, my name was almost erased and then gradually rebuilt to mean "servant of God and others," "encourager", and "one who empowers others."

The real test, of course, came when I was set free. So many people "get religion" in prison and then prove false to its power once they are released. Gladly, that was not the case for me. I continued to strengthen myself on God's word and to focus on how I could help others.

I've found it to be exactly as Jesus promised in Acts 20:35, "There is more happiness in giving than there is in receiving."

My first stop was the Alston Wilkes Federal Halfway House in Columbia, South Carolina. All federal prisoners are required to stay at a halfway house until they get a job or get on their feet. I stayed for two months and focused on helping the other residents. My motto was: We can do this!

Interestingly enough, three years later, they hired me to work as a Behavioral Interventionist. I was getting paid to do the very things that I did naturally when I was a resident there.

In the meantime, within a month of being released from prison, I landed a job with GANG OUT. My background as a former officer with specialized training with gangs and my experience as a former inmate was a perfect match for young people who were involved in gangs. This organization worked in the schools to discourage gang involvement and to help current gang members extract themselves safely. I absolutely loved helping young people make better choices.

When funding for the job dried up in 2010, I became Campus Director for the local Boys & Girls Club. Through a glitch in the application process—which I credit to Divine intervention—it was not discovered that I was a former inmate until eight months into the program. By this time, I had nearly doubled the enrollment in the Boys & Girls Club of the Midlands in Columbia, South Carolina because my activities were fun. Kids were telling their buddies to sign up and they were also spreading the word at their schools.

When my fingerprints were finally processed, the organization could see that I was a transformed man and they kept me on. Alston Wilkes Society then hired me in 2011 at a significant pay raise. This allowed me to keep helping people in need—just BIGGER people.

Then, in 2012, I was hired by a local elementary school as the Expectations Coach and Director of the After School Program—because of my proven ability to reach children and have a positive impact on their lives. This is my current and my favorite job—redirecting young lives where it can really make a difference.

Both Side of the Bars

Forty-Seven

Giving Back

There's work and then there's personal time. Even though I've loved nearly every job I've ever had—and really poured my heart into it—I still wanted to do more. I wanted to spend personal time helping others help themselves.

My opportunity came just two months after I stepped into freedom. In an effort to keep my spirituality alive, I went to a non-denominational prayer meeting. About 75 people showed up. According to my research, the purpose of the group was to look at current issues—world hunger, crime in our town, poverty, and such—and then pray for a solution.

However, at my first meeting, one of the attendees asked the group to pray for her personally. She was going through a tough time and needed strength. She stood in the middle and the group surrounded her. It was understood that whoever felt called would pray.

One person prayed. Then a second. Next, a third. And then—dead silence. Thoughts whirled through my mind. Here is this hurting lady, in the middle of 75 people and that's it? So, though I had no prior intention of praying, I felt like I had to come to her rescue. So I prayed—something—I really don't know what.

Well, while I was praying, she looked around so she could remember me. Then, after the meeting she smiled and said, "I'm Gladys Grimaud. You prayed about something that only God and I knew about. Who are you?"

I raised my eyebrows and smiled as I said, "I'm Anthony Bryant."

She said, "Do you have a home church?"

I said, "No, I'm looking around."

Long story short, I eventually visited her church. After the service, I met her husband Joe, a retired Air Force colonel, and they took me to lunch. Once they heard my story and my passion to help others, they opened doors for me start speaking at the local homeless shelter and the Youth Detention Center in Columbia, South Carolina. In time, they became like a mother and a father to me—always ready to listen, to mentor, and to support my dreams.

Initially, I used my lunch break to zip over to the homeless shelter to give them a hand up. I delivered my presentations in way that would spark a ray of hope, empower a forward step, or bring some joy to a dismal situation.

The youth at the detention center were a whole different crowd. They were street smart and tough. Plenty of people came to "talk," but they awarded me "street credit" because I'd done that and been there—to prison and back.

I gave back to the community by speaking at the homeless shelter and the Youth Detention Center. I continue to speak and reach out to youth—inspiring them turn their lives around early. I give them the tools to accomplish their goals.

We talked about good choices and bad choices. We talked about the long term and sometimes lifetime consequences that come from split-second decisions. I've stuck with this group for over eight years now and it's almost like we are family.

In fact, sometimes I'll take an inspiring movie—like Facing Your Giants—and we eat popcorn, watch the movie, and then have rap session on what it all means.

I'm hoping and praying that someday, one of these young people will walk up to me in the grocery store and say, "Mr. Bryant, I heard what you said. I did what you suggested. And, I turned my life around. Thank you for caring enough to keep coming back."

From my initial volunteer speaking engagements came more. I've worked both as a paid and an unpaid speaker/ trainer in churches, schools, colleges, and with law enforcement agencies.

My greatest joy is found in training law enforcement agencies. However, I still speak at youth events—empowering students to make healthy choices.

10 Commandments for Success as a Young Person

1.) **Love, listen to, and respect your parent(s).** It is easy to forget the sacrifices our parents or caregivers have made for us. It is vitally important to be thankful for all that they have and will do for us.

2.) **Pick your friends wisely.** There is a New Testament verse that says, "Bad company corrupts good morals." (1 Corinthians 15:33) In my life, when I had good friends, they brought out the best in me. When I switched to friends with low moral values—I dropped my values and ended up spending 10 years in federal prison.

3.) **No drugs or illegal substances.** These things are self-destructive. They will never make you better or more mature. They will give you the illusion of control, while robbing you of your future power and opportunities.

4.) **Education.** Do obtain your high school diploma, GED, or other form of higher education, such as a college degree, vocational certification, or license. Make yourself more useful and productive by investing in your skills.

5.) **Maintain a positive mental attitude.** Surround yourself with positive people and music. Stay away from negative minded people who will "zap" or drain your energy and zest for achieving your personal goals.

6.) **Obey the law.** My mother said, "Trouble is easy to get into and hard to get out of." She was 100% right. I had to learn the hard way. You can learn from my experience.

7.) Cultivate endurance. We live in a highly competitive world. Develop the inner strength to withstand stress, perform at peak level even under pressure, and most of all, to recover and try again when you have a setback. The only losers are those who quit.

8.) Network. Establish a network of friends who are like-minded and already doing what you want to do. Look for people who accept personal responsibility, have a plan, are willing to help and ask for help, and who want to see you succeed.

9.) Stay focused. No matter how it looks from your vantage point, no one has an easy life. Focus on having a meaningful life and expect that you will have to work for it. Create a goal board by pasting pictures of what you want (car, job, college, mountain bike, friends, pet, etc.) on the board and then hang it in your room. Every night, look at it and remind yourself of what you are aiming for. It will help you stay focused when problems arise.

10.) Eat healthy, exercise, and sleep. A healthy diet, regular exercise, and getting 8 or more hours of sleep does more than keep our bodies fit. These things contribute to our mental and emotional health. In short—we feel better, even happier. We have more to give to others.

10 Commandments for Surviving Parenthood

As the Expectations Coach and Director of an After School Program—I've been called upon to gather parenting resources and to present parenting programs for larger groups. Here is an outline of best practices.

1.) **Define your rules and principles.** Once you know what your rules are, clarify and communicate with your child. Children need to hear what you believe, loud and clear. It is a mistake to make up rules along the way or to have constantly changing rules.

2.) **Love your children and spend time with them.** You can never say, "I love you" too many times to a child. However, besides words, we need to show love in action. We can do this by attending her sports events, playing with them, or teaching them a skill. Don't try to buy love with gifts. Their favorite present is your presence.

3.) **Use motivating words.** Instead of telling your child he did a job poorly, try saying, "I need you to do it this way." Then, demonstrate the better way. Also, compliment a child on what they do (not on how they look) and when they display values such as honesty, good work ethic, or generosity—praise them. When a child is struggling, reassure him or her by saying, "I believe in you. I know you can do this." Words are powerful.

4.) **Listen to their side of the story.** Hearing their story is a sign of respect. When we listen to our children, they are more likely to listen to us. And, when children see that we really care about them, then, they are ready to hear our insights. Also, encourage your child to contribute to the solution by asking, "What do you think about this? What are you going to do to prevent this from happening again?"

5.) Praise good behavior. Catch your child doing something good and praise him or her for it. It will reinforce the positive behavior. Say, "I appreciate you cleaning your room, washing the dishes, or feeding the dog."

6.) Negotiate. Decide in advance which behaviors are negotiable. Negotiable issues can be curfews, television time, or WHEN to do homework (before or after dinner). Non-negotiable rules involve safety, health, homework completion, and good manners. Remember, as children grow the rules need to grow with them.

7.) Be realistic. What is non-negotiable at one age can be negotiable when a child is older. Consider your child's friends, personality, and environment. If your child now wants more control over clothing or hair styles—you may be able to be flexible as long as it does not go against your moral or family code. Give independence gradually.

8.) DON'T Scream. Remember, if you lose you temper you've lost the battle. Instead, when tempers start to flare, give yourself a time out. Talk about issues when you and your child are calm. Then, when the issue is resolved—treat the two of you to a favorite snack.

9.) DON'T Make Snap Decisions. In the heat of the moment, parents at times will make arbitrary decisions that are hard to reverse or follow through on. For example, "I'm going to ground you for a year" is usually not what we really want to do. When we speak impulsively and cannot follow through, it weakens our authority and we lose our child's respect. Instead, once again, take a time out. And, when you make a mistake, admit it. Tell your child, "Wow. I made a bad decision. I'm sorry. Let me take some time to sort this out and I will get back with you." Then, when you have made a decision, first say, "I know you feel bad for what you did. We all make mistakes and the goal is to learn from them so that we don't do it again. Now, because you did what you did, here is your consequence." Allow the child to own the behavior and the resulting consequence.

10.)   DON'T Confuse Discipline and Punishment. Discipline is about guiding children in ways that support their development of self-control. It is a way of training people to obey a code of behavior. Discipline is respectful, accepting, comforting, and builds self-worth. Punishment is intended to hurt the child and focuses on the child rather than on the behavior. Punishment is often used when parents feel frustrated, angry, or hurt. It sends the message, "You are a bad child." This destroys self-esteem, trust, and the parent-child bond. So, if a child talks back or throws a temper tantrum—instead of reacting in anger—try to think of how you can teach your child new skills to share their feelings in respectful manner. For starters, calmly give them the consequence, "Go to your room and we will talk when you are calmed down." Then, demonstrate what respectful talk sounds like versus the "back talk" that the child used. In this way, the child can literally hear the difference. Proper discipline opens the lines of communication by removing the roadblocks in a respectful manner.

Both Side of the Bars

Forty-Eight

Lessons Learned

When I look back at my choice to become involved in an illegal activity at the age of 29, I realized that it was not due to a split-second decision. It was the result of several split-second decisions that—repeated often enough—reset the markers on my value system.

For instance, when the seasoned shift officer drank a beer in front of me and then offered me a beer—I had to make a split second decision. At that time, my value markers were set at a high level. I believed in following the rules.

So, a little bell went off in my head yelling, "Warning. Warning. It is against departmental policy to drink alcohol eight hours before reporting for duty. It is important to follow the rules. I am a role model."

I did some quick mental math and it was only four hours until we started our shift. Clearly, drinking a beer would be the wrong choice.

However, another little bell went off. "Warning. Warning. This is a test. Are you a team player? Can I count on you to have my back?"

So now, I was at my first crossroads of compromise. In my mind—in this split second—I had to make the choice. One—I could obey the letter of the policy—and that would result in the blessing of the agency, but most likely I would be ostracized by my fellow officers.

Two—I could break the "law"—and the agency would probably never find out anyways. After all, this officer was doing it and probably had been for years. And, there was a huge pay off. If I chose to imitate him—I'd get huge points in trust and be accepted as part of the team. I would be invited to more cookouts and other cool activities.

Obviously, I chose choice two. I took the beer. But I didn't just take the beer once. I drank beer repeatedly before reporting on duty. Over time, I did this so much—my marker moved so low—that the warning bell stopped bugging me.

The problem is, once I crossed that line—deciding for myself what is right and wrong—I began to lose perspective. The lines really started to get blurry, because self-interest began to dominate my thoughts. It was no longer what's best for the department or what's best for my family—it was what is best for Anthony.

The next major crossroads came when I was pressured by my peers to have an extramarital affair. I tried to buy time by making up fantasy affairs, but the time came when I was pushed make a decision.

When I think back on it, they probably ganged up on me intentionally—but they cornered me at a barbeque and told me that a lady in the Sheriff's office was asking about me.

They said, "She's interested in you, man. What are you going to do?"

In a split-second, I had to make a decision. I'd already fabricated a house of lies and they were going to push on it to see if it would topple.

That little bell rang out, "Warning. Warning. You love your wife. You have been faithful to her and she has been faithful to you. You don't want to break that trust. You don't want to hurt Red."

However, as the guys' eyes burned holes in my back, I also heard the other call. "Warning. Warning. This is a test. Are you your own man? Are you one of us? Can we count on you to cover for us with our girlfriends? We need a little dirt on you as an insurance policy."

I didn't have much time to wrestle with this. But ultimately it was a choice of loyalty. Was I going to be loyal to Red or to my fellow officers?

"Give her my telephone number," I told them with a smile.

In hindsight, though, I didn't just have an affair or two or three. With the affair came a value marker so low that I could lie, steal, and cheat. It came with the territory. To cover my affairs, I had to lie to Red about where I was and what I was doing.

In having an affair, I was stealing sex from someone else's wife or someone's unmarried daughter. Whatever the case, I didn't have a marriage contract with her, so she wasn't mine.

And, I was cheating. I was cheating Red out of what she deserved. I did have a contract with her—written, spoken, and heart to heart—that I would reserve my sexual self for her and her alone.

This was the perfect seedbed for greed. Once I broke free from my moral code—my value markers—I wanted more and more pleasure, freedom, and power. Pretty soon, there ceased to be a crossroads. I just did what I felt like doing.

I would even drink and drive. Now, how crazy is that. By day—I was arresting drunk drivers under the illusion that I was being a hero and protecting my community. But by night—I was driving under the influence—deluding myself that somehow I could do it better and safer than the average citizen.

When you add in a huge dose of entitlement—officers don't arrest officers or blow the whistle on them—you have Superman gone crazy.

I have to say that in retrospect—I was on the wrong path and sliding down hill fast. For years, I blamed my brother for what he asked me to do. But when I really did some soul searching, I realized that if not him—something else likely would have snared me.

That is why I can speak so powerfully to the law enforcement brotherhood. Major compromise is the result of one small and repeated compromise after another. It is rarely, if ever, a single giant step. It is caused by the gradual erosion of our ethics.

Ethics

Ethics are the moral principles that govern our behavior. What we have to remember is that they can change or erode over time. It is so gradual that it may sneak up on us. So, we need to keep double-checking our value markers.

Oversimplified, ethics could be summed up in, "Don't lie, don't steal, don't cheat." Broadened a bit, we could add the golden rule: "Always treat others the way that you would want to be treated." So in a highly ethical relationship of any kind, we would always be encouraging the highest standard of behavior in others and they in us.

Relating this to law enforcement—officers are expected to have the highest moral, ethical, and professional standards. When an officer or other public official of trust breaks these standards, the community holds them 10 times more accountable. Why? They promise—they are sworn in—to maintain the highest ethics. In return, they are given a tremendous amount of power, authority, freedom, and responsibility. So when they fall—they get very little sympathy, compassion, or forgiveness for corruption.

When I was in prison, I came across dozens of "high profile" inmates. These were professionals with great jobs— lawyers, accountants, doctors, officers, professors, pastors, senators, and judges. I would always ask them: "What contributed to your unethical decision?"

LOVE of Money

I know this, because I caught the disease myself. It's not that money is bad. It's not. It is when greed sets in. In an effort to get more than you can earn—you look for ways to break the rules. Personally, I loved money to a fault. I loved what it did for my life. I could buy status, security, and pleasure. The sky was the limit. All I needed was more money.

Pretty soon, the more I had, the more I wanted. No. Actually, it went from a want to a need. Somehow, my happiness depended on having more. When that mental switch was thrown, I started behaving like an addict.

Once those FBI scenarios started happening—and I was paid $2500 for an hour's work, making more in a hour than I made in a month on my job—I was hooked. At that point, all my ethics and "sworn to serve" went out the window. Anthony was looking out for Anthony.

Financial Pressures

This is different from the love of money. Love of money is ME chasing money. Financial pressure is BILLS chasing me. When I was living beyond my means, I was actually creating new debt at the very time when I had an abundance of cash.

When the burden of debt began to weigh heavy on me—I looked for a way to escape. Engaging in unethical practices seemed to be a quick and easy solution.

Part of the problem was financial illiteracy. When I was in school, we were never taught how to save and manage money—even though it is a critical life skill. So, I let money flow in and out of my hands like a never ending river. However, it became a problem when my cash flow remained constant and my plastic spending began to escalate. Eventually, those "minimum payments" kept going up until they were a maximum burden.

Peer Pressure

Wikipedia dictionary states, "Peer pressure is influence a peer group, observers, or an individual exerts that encourages others to change their attitudes, values, or behaviors to conform to those of the influencing group or individual".

In the FBI sting, some of the individuals did state their unethical decision was influenced by a co-worker, friend, or someone they respected and trusted.

Dr. Jonathan Caspi wrote an article noting "*It is an odd thought that our sibling relationships may be at the center of what makes us who we become. We may prefer to say that our success is due to parental support, social connections, and particularly our personal attributes, including our own hard work and intelligence. However, it is our siblings that may be the most influential in this regard. They shape our sense of selves, our identities, our skill sets, and ultimately our life choices*". The love, respect, and trust I had (and still do) for my brother did greatly influence my ultimate decision to take part in an unethical act.

However, as I mentioned earlier—it was peer pressure from my fellow officers that started me down the slippery slope of ethical compromise.

After being released from prison, I went to visit my brother, Tommy.

He is hopeful that he will be released soon.

Ego Trip

Lord Acton, a British historian said, "Power corrupts and absolute power corrupts absolutely." He was observing that a person's sense of morality can decrease as power bestowed upon him increases.

I can attest to this personally. As an officer, I fell victim to the "Superman Complex." With all my newfound authority, weapon, and fast car—I started feeling invincible. I could see clearly the phenomenal power behind the badge and the uniform. Beautiful women threw themselves at my feet like I was some kind of a god, while angry lion-like men calmed into purring kittens when I approached.

Pretty soon, I thought I was special. I thought I could live above the very law that I was hired to uphold. To add to my delusion—fellow cops covered for me. And, I covered for the other officers, politicians, and high ranking officials. When I pulled them over for a DUI—I let these Supermen arrange for someone to pick them up—without issuing a ticket. With all these perks—free movies, free food, ticket-free living—I had an ego the size of a basketball and a sense of entitlement as deep as the Pocomoke River.

Lessons Learned

The ROOTS of

My Identity

At the start of my career

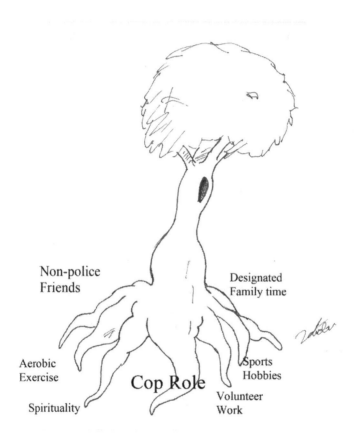

Non-police
Friends

Designated
Family time

Aerobic
Exercise

Sports
Hobbies

Cop Role

Volunteer
Work

Spirituality

The ROOTS of

My Identity

As my career progresses

Cop Role

We do it to ourselves. We slowly chop off the roots of our core identity. We falsely believe that this will make us a stronger, better, more committed cop.

Both Side of the Bars

Forty-Nine

The REAL Cost of My Choices

Prison gave me 10 years and four months to think about the consequences of my unethical choice. Here is what I concluded.

Personal Impact

Choosing to "aid and abet" was the most self-destructive decision I have ever made in my life. Now, when I was actually participating—I was sufficiently drugged by my greed and ego that I was feeling no pain at all. But when I was arrested and put in the national spotlight—I sobered up quickly and was shocked at my own behavior.

My exposed failure was the root cause of the most horrific major depression and suicidal thoughts during the first year of my incarceration. I lost my dignity, my self-worth, and even my name. I was no longer Officer Anthony Bryant, but now inmate #09589-021.

In place of my street clothes—which I had invested $1000s over the former 10 years—I was forced to wear an ill-fitting uniform. These clothes were constant reminders of my shame, guilt, and loss. My losses added up to loss of job, loss of family, loss of freedom, and loss of self.

Marital Impact

Red divorced me two years into my sentence. At first, I was angry with her for "abandoning" me at the lowest point in my life. Later, I took a closer look at the whole situation and put the blame where it belonged—on ME. I realized that I abandoned her a few years earlier—finding new lovers—and so why should she wait on me? She was a beautiful, wholesome, loyal 28-year-old woman that had every right to get on with her life.

Just for those who think that if they went to prison, their spouses would wait for them, this is what the experts say: An online article titled *Prison Marriage* cited a study as follows: *"The divorce rate among couples where one spouse is incarcerated for one year or more is 80% for men and close to 100% for women."*

I realized that my unethical decision jeopardized the health, happiness, and livelihood of my life, my wife, and my children.

Impact on Children

I was no dummy. I did my research and what I found out almost killed me. Studies show that children who grow up with an incarcerated parent (especially the father) are twice as likely to come to prison, join a gang, and if female, get pregnant at an early age.

My children were going to spend virtually all of their childhood without me. My daughter would be 22 and my son would be 16 when I completed my 10 year term.

Also, seeing my mom crying in the courtroom—feeling the pain of all of my family that I hurt—was nearly unbearable.

I asked my children to write me a letter explaining what it was like through their eyes to have their dad in prison. Here is what Tranise wrote.

Letter from my Daughter—2016

Before I begin, don't take what I'm about to say to heart. I'm only giving you what you asked for. Also, I want it to be known that everything that I say is to not be manipulated and is to be disclosed verbatim. If you choose not to comply, I request that you don't include me in this book.

Honestly, I didn't want to write this. But being that my father felt that it would be a good read for his book and I had not really had a conversation about what happened and how his actions affected us (my brother and I), I've agreed to participate. I'm not one to block someone's blessings, so if this is one of the ways God chooses to bless you, then so be it.

I was young when it happened, middle school age, and I remember hearing my parents waking up early in the morning. My father opened the door. I heard distress and worry in my mother's voice.

I heard the officers speaking calmly, as though they didn't want to disturb or wake anyone up, as the sound of handcuffs clicked around my father's wrist. My mother guided me back to my room and told me to stay there. I peeped through the blinds of my window to see what was going on and watched in disbelief as my father was being taken away in a cop car.

Being young and confused, I was mad. I was asking questions to myself, wondering how dare they come and take my dad away from us? Don't they know he's a Deputy Sheriff? Little did I know, from this point on, my life would never be the same.

I am very reserved when it comes to my personal life so I figured, let me just make it through the day. No one knows what's going on, but one day as I was taking my seat in class, my home room teacher grabbed a newspaper and immediately took me outside of the class room. I remember the stares and looks on people's faces as this was happening.

She closed the door behind us, showed me the newspaper, and I immediately began to cry. I already knew what it was she was trying to get me to see. She just wanted to make sure that I was ok. That was the day when I realized, without realizing, that I had to grow up. That day is when I learned how to suppress my feelings so that I can appear strong so that I don't have anyone feeling sorry for me.

It didn't take me long to master this. Because of this numbness, I've learned not only how to be strong, but how to be strong for my mother and little brother.

I remember my little brother asking for daddy when he wasn't there and how my mom tried to hold it together. She tried to explain to us what was happening. Eventually she broke down. I remember cleaning up her vomit from off the bathroom floor and her face. I helped her get in the bed because the situation made her sick to her stomach.

I remember her losing her job and working at Waffle House because it was hard to find a job. I remember having to move in with our grandma because my mom made the decision to sacrifice time with us so that she could join the military to better our lives.

I remember becoming sexually active at the age of 14 because I was bored, with no guidance, and unknowingly angry inside because we had to be without our mother and father. Thus, leaving me to seek the love and attention my father was giving me when he was around.

I remember driving through two states with my little brother by ourselves at the age of 16, nervous and angry that we had to stop our lives to go see our father in prison. Still having to be strong so that my brother won't feel any negativity towards my father.

I remember phone calls from my father and finally realizing that he was mainly calling to keep tabs on my mom, because he would be more concerned about what was going on in the background that he'd lose track of what he was talking about.

I can go on and on for years about how my father's bad decision impacted our lives drastically, but I've suppressed so many memories of those moments that they've become the root to my anger and passive aggressive personality.

By the way did I mention how my father, to this day, still has not had an open and genuine conversation about how this made us feel and affected us. Maybe that's why he doesn't have a real connection because he's too busy still trying to prove himself and to create this image to be socially accepted. Maybe after he puts our side of the story in his book and he does well on sells, he'll realize how much hurt we've endured and he will want to talk about it. Until then, I'll patiently wait.

I hope this is what you were looking for and I pray that your book does well. I'll love you always.

"Don't wait around for other people to be happy for you. Any happiness you get, you've got to make yourself." ~ Alice Walker
{Tranise Hasan}

Letter from my Son—2016
Growing Up without my Dad

It wouldn't be anything new to talk about my life without a father figure present as a black male in America. Sadly, the stereotype is all too common among our people. At 4 years old, my dad didn't willfully leave me but was "taken away" for a crime he committed.

His decisions were of his own choice but the consequences and effects of his actions not only affected his life but his family's as well. To note, this is not a note of hate, regret, anger, or resentment, but an honest listing of some personal experiences, thoughts, and recollections of a black male learning to be a man.

Dad arrested at age 4
Dad released at age 16

Personality

A lot can happen in 12 years. This time frame was probably the best years of influence towards my personality and morals. Unfortunately, I was only able to take on one role model, that being my mother. She did an amazing job but I believe it to be true that a woman cannot teach a boy how to fully be a man.

I grew up on what most people would call a "reserved" side. I was kind, respectful, caring, honest, and disciplined. By witnessing my mom's struggle prior to and after joining the military, I became ambitious and self-motivated to want better for myself and family coming from two families that lacked positive role-models. During my teenage years, I grew up in neighborhoods that didn't have many kids to interact with, so my social growth was slow but I eventually got there.

Interests

I'm weird, but not in a bad way. I'm different from the "box" of what every black man should be interested in or doing. Growing up mostly around my mother's side of the family I was surrounded by women for the majority of my childhood. I enjoyed spending time with my male cousin (Jabree) but without a father or much male influence, growing up I didn't take to the typical actions and behaviors that a boy should be exhibiting at a certain age.

As a kid, I was actively outside playing with other kids daily, but during pre-teen years, I found an interest in music, art, anime, video games, and other outlets that didn't require much interaction with others. I sometimes think that if my dad was there, I might have been in a sport or at least more interested in them. I like the idea of having a team and being raised to follow and support said team or to grill and even learn how to "hang with the fellas."

Relationships & Dating

Again, a woman cannot teach a boy how to fully be a man. Discovering my interests, my sexual arousals, and ultimately my gender specific anatomy on my own was rough. Waking up and not knowing what was going on, but having no one to speak to about it; wondering how to talk to women without coming off as awkward or rude; or even sex and what I could expect to happen throughout the action.

It was all self-taught or learned by means of research and observation. While other men have learned these life lessons without a father figure as well, some that I've interacted with have mentioned that they had "their boys," an uncle, or honestly just went out and experimented. I never went out and recklessly started experimenting, but I definitely had a delay in putting myself out there to date with no direction or instruction.

Even now, I'm not one to aggressively chase after a relationship. I feel like growing up without a dad or male figure to explain what was going on during my adolescence left me in a mild state of confusion, where I had to pick up on things as a man on my own or through a computer screen.

Overall, children are born from two parents (male &female) for a reason; to influence, to nurture, and to teach. Without input from both, a child can potentially miss out on life lessons and a connection to the one that is missing.

I turned out to be a great son, despite some personal issues that I have gone through, but I am glad and fortunate to have a father that wants to still be a part of my life. I was never picked on for not having a dad. Honestly, the topic rarely came up and if it did it, his status was mentioned and left at that.

My life could have been better or worse with a father figure present but that's just life so I play with the hand I'm dealt. I love my dad and will always appreciate and respect him. We've still got plentyof years to make up for but it's all in due time!

Public Impact

The public was outraged by our misuse of trust and power. With all the negative media attention—and a fanning of the flames with a hot news item—people began to use a broad brush to paint "all" officers in Savannah, Georgia as corrupt. So my behavior caused disgrace and even consequences for hundreds of innocent law enforcement officers.

Due to public outcry, there were major changes in structure and leadership. Whole units were branded as corrupt due to the actions and choices of a handful of officers.

10 Commandments of Cop Survival

The uniform, badge, and gun are highly visible symbols of power and authority. When an officer wears these, he automatically inherits the authority that goes with it. The officer commands obedience, respect, and control from the public. This is known as "police personality." While it is necessary on the job—remember to take it off when you step out of your uniform and into family, social, or private life.

1.) Don't be a blabber mouth. The officer that "sees all, tells all" quickly becomes ostracized by fellow officers. There is nothing worse than an officer with diarrhea of the mouth. There is an unwritten "code of silence" that demands officers to cover for an officer in trouble on the job or with their spouse or girlfriend/boyfriend, whether or not the knowing officer agrees with the behavior.

2.) Brotherhood AND Family. There is a tendency to believe that you must put the police brotherhood ahead of your family. After all, you must rely on fellow officers in life and death situations. However, it is possible—and necessary for a balanced life—to have a powerful connection with the brotherhood without sidelining your family. Set aside designated time to spend with your family and hold yourself to your commitment. Family is important.

3.) Leave work alive. While on duty, it is your job to make sure that you come home alive and well so that you can go to work another day to protect the community. Protect yourself.

4.) Beware of us vs. them. Officers have to see human behavior at its worst. It doesn't matter if you are working the rich side of town or the poor side, you soon see that all sides have problems. Because of this, it is easy to develop a cynical and untrusting attitude—believing that police are the only ones that have their lives together. When you see this happening, realize that you need to spend more time with non-police friends, hobbies, sports, spirituality and other endeavors that restore your faith in humanity.

5.) Wait for back up. One of the easiest ways to increase your safety and chances of success is to wait for your back up. Don't try to be the lone ranger.

6.) Expect the unexpected. No call is routine. Be prepared and alert for anything. Complacency is the enemy. A relaxed attitude could cause harm to you or your fellow officer.

7.) Always wear your vest. It may be hot and it may be uncomfortable—but a vest is never optional. The day you don't wear it could be the one day you really need it.

8.) Trust your instincts. It you don't think something is right, it's probably not. It is better to be safe than to be sorry.

9.) NEVER eat fast food via the drive-through window. It is a fact that employees will deliberately tamper with an officer's meal if they feel distain for law enforcement. Take the extra effort to park your car and walk inside.

10.) Be professional and courteous at all times. A law enforcement officer is a role model. Therefore, your private and professional life is always being evaluated.

Both Side of the Bars

Fifty

The Truth About Police

Like many officers, I operated under the misconception that I had to make moral compromises to buy into the team. Additionally, I thought that I had to spend large amounts of time away from my family—so I could bond and build loyalty with my police family.

That's simply not true. I want to introduce you to my partner and friend, Officer Tommie Simpson Osborne of the Chatham County Police Department. She recently retired after a long and successful career in law enforcement. Here is how she navigated the obstacles and temptations that throw so many officers off balance.

Officer Tommie Simpson Osborne's Story

Officer Tommie Simpson Osborne did policing right.

She was an excellent officer who managed to keep her professional life and her personal life balanced.

Both Side of the Bars

Being a law enforcement officer is not an easy job. I started out as a Corrections Officer with Anthony Bryant, but then was hired by the Chatham County Police Department in 1995. Since that time, I've personally known of five officers who committed suicide. I worked with three of them on the street.

Officer Willie Phillips worked with us as a Corrections Officer before becoming a police officer and he hung himself. It could have been the stress of the job. There is plenty of internal politics in law enforcement agencies. Or, it could have been personal problems.

A Sergeant on my watch shot himself at home. They found a note in his patrol car. Everyone was shocked because the week we attended his funeral, he was supposed to be attending his wedding. I worked with him and I never would have guessed that he was depressed or stressed out.

Officer Michael Broome was an undercover cop. He was having problems with his wife. They divorced and then he started stalking her. After his second arrest for stalking, he was fired. So, he checked himself out. That was in 2011.

In 2014, Lt. Andre Oliver shot himself in his car. His Chief of Police Willie Lovett was sentenced to seven years in federal prison the following year for corruption. It was believed that Oliver was involved and afraid that it would come out—so he shot himself in his car.

Then, on Memorial Day—May 30, 2016—Lieutenant Jeff Olson, the officer who trained Anthony, shot himself. He was the commander for the Hostage Negotiation Team (SWAT) for the Savannah-Chatham Metropolitan Police Department. No one saw that coming.

I found police work to be very demanding and sometimes extremely stressful, too. But, I found a way to manage it. First, I viewed it as a job. This is key, because so many officers, especially young officers, view it as their identity. So, when anything threatens their "identity" they can overreact or ultimately check themselves out.

Actually, I always told myself that I had two jobs. I was a police officer and I was a mother. When I left the one job, I fully immersed myself in the other.

Because of that mindset, I was able to resist cop culture. The dark side of cop culture includes alcohol, adultery, cloaking, and agency politics.

Alcohol

When it came to drinking with the team—before or after work—I just didn't do it. The fact is, this did NOT affect the trust level between me and the other officers.

On the downside—if I wanted to be a part of the "officer's club"—then the choice to abstain from drinking with co-workers would put the brakes on that. But my choice was to keep work as work and to use my off-duty time be the best mother I could possibly be, build friendships with non-officers, engage in hobbies, and stay active in my church.

I have heard of officers who were able to walk a fine line of doing both. They could have ONE drink with the team after work and then go home. This seemed to keep everyone happy— the police family and the home family.

Adultery

Before I started working in law enforcement—even as a corrections officer—I dated a guy. Later, he became a police officer. Then, he started cheating on me, so I broke it off. After that, I've never dated an officer and I never dated where I worked.

Within a short time of being hired as a police officer, I saw that cheating is just part of the culture. It doesn't matter if it's the Chief, the supervisors, the officers, or the staff—adultery is accepted and expected.

I remember one officer who had a goal of having sex with every new female who was hired into the department. Amazingly, he usually met his goal. With the exception of myself, I'm not aware of any other female officer who held her ground against him. I know for me, he propositioned me repeatedly, but I just kept turning him down.

It also shocked me to see how many officers had children outside their marriage. Even though it might be a career killer in other professions—its commonly accepted in law enforcement.

On the street—people virtually throw themselves at your uniform. When I see that happening, I'm quick to say, "I'm married." Of course, a lot of them will say, "So what. So am I." So the temptation is being dangled in front of you all the time. This makes it a challenge to be loyal to your spouse or even to yourself.

On the other end of the spectrum, police officers who join the "officers club" face tremendous peer pressure to cheat on their mates. They actually have competitions to see how many different women they can get under their belt in a given period of time. It's all consensual sex—but it erodes self-respect,

respect for women (police work is male dominated and mostly heterosexual), respect for the family, and respect for the community officers are supposed to be serving and protecting.

I think with this behavior—there is a bit of a belief that police are naturally risk takers. They live on the wild side. And, after all, who wants a toothless sheepdog protecting the flock of citizens. So, it becomes "accepted" that this is "normal" cop behavior that has to be "managed" and controlled, but not removed.

However, in my time, I think that this pattern of adultery could eventually cause consequence that are too difficult to bear—resulting in painful family break ups and sometimes even suicide.

Cloaking

I believe that if you are living right—as a cop—then you don't need anyone to cloak (cover up) for you. Even if you make a mistake—you can own it and fix it. That is the way that I operated as an officer.

That having been said, I did learn to look the other way. When I was on detective duty, my partner and I were called out with a warrant for a guy. When we arrived at the scene, the suspect was already in handcuffs. One of the male officers took the butt of his gun and hit the suspect right in the face. Excessive force? You bet. My partner and I walked away. We refused to witness that. There were supervisors present and they saw what we saw. We didn't volunteer anything.

Cloaking goes a step farther. IF I'd been asked about what I saw and IF I lied to protect the officer instead of the suspect, that would be cloaking. Usually, it happened like this, though. My partner has an affair and his wife calls me to confirm her suspicions. I know all about it, because my partner has been bragging for weeks.

However, when his wife calls, I say, "I don't know anything about that. I don't know what you're talking about."

I can raise the cloak higher by adding, "Actually, he's been over to my house playing cards on the last two Wednesday nights. So, he couldn't have been with anyone else."

Cloaking gets really sad when officers beat their wives. Yes, domestic violence is a problem in all professions and especially in high stress jobs like law enforcement. Imagine the powerless wife who can't get anyone to "protect" her because the police department is too busy protecting itself. That's sad.

Agency Politics

A tremendous amount of power and authority is granted to officers when they are hired. For me, when I was in my patrol car protecting my assigned side of town—I was my own boss. In other words—no one was breathing down my neck. No supervisor was in my car micromanaging me. I was trusted to make decisions within seconds to protect others and to protect myself.

However, when I stepped into the agency—it was like stepping into the military. Within the agency—my supervisor is the boss and it's my job to follow orders. I am really powerless to pick my position or do what I think is best for me or the community.

One time, after working a certain side of town for some time—I was arbitrarily moved to another side of town. What's the problem with that? On my side of town—I've built relationships. I know what "normal" looks like and I can readily spot when something's up. I know who I can count on in my section of the community.

Changing my assignment to another side of town— sometimes more dangerous than my current assignment—means I'm going to be at a disadvantage while I'm learning the new ropes. The frustrating aspect of this is that sometimes it's a matter of officers and supervisors playing favorites and there is nothing I can do to address the problem.

I remember one time, I submitted a request for vacation time well in advance. I had a good reason for wanting that time. However, the higher ups—knowing I wanted this—gave it to someone else. Sometimes, it almost seemed like they were purposely rattling my cage.

Also, the paperwork and reports that must be done in police work can be overwhelming. Sometimes officers get a supervisor that keeps sending the report back because literally a "t" was not crossed. Rotating shifts is another problem. It comes with the territory—it is part of the culture—but it sure takes its toll on your sleep and your family when your shift keeps changing.

In the final analysis—I had to come to grips with the reality that officers have very little control over their careers. They can be trained, moved, find their sweet spot and then moved to their "worst" option—all within the legitimate rights of hierarchy.

So, in the end, what I as an officer can control is my professionalism. I can get a degree. In fact, I earned three degrees while serving as an officer—a bachelor's in criminology, a master's in counseling, and EDS in leadership.

I can control my level of personal integrity, trust, honesty, willingness to serve and sacrifice and all the other qualities we look for in genuine role models. In the end, I can control me.

A Snapshot of my Life

When I applied to be a Corrections Officer, the administrator said doubtfully, "You've worked at a convenience store, you've been a bus driver, and currently you're a bank teller. I don't think you have what it takes to make a good officer."

I completed my training at the Academy anyways, took my first job as a corrections officer from 1992-1995, and then was hired on with the Chatham County Police Department.

I took the job to pay my bills. As a divorced single mom with three children—one with muscular dystrophy—I needed to get the financial part of my life locked in.

I went to work every day giving my best and knowing that I had three children counting on me to come home. So, I took advantage of all the training I could get. If anyone was coming home in a body bag, it wasn't going to be me.

I followed the rules—always waiting for back up. I followed the chain of command. I looked out for my partner and really did my best to serve and protect the community as fiercely as I protected my own children.

As soon as I was off-duty, I put myself on-duty as a mother. Now I have to back up here for a moment. Police work requires officers to amp up to a higher level of awareness, often called hypervigilance. It's a high state of energy that helps officers detect little signals of "what's wrong" so that they can derail dangerous situations.

Staying in the hypervigilant state for 8-12 hours while on duty, can make it difficult to wind down and operate in "normal" mode. For me, when I got home from work—regardless if I'd pulled first, second, or third shift—I felt hyper and exhausted at the same time. So, my first action when I walked in the door was to head to my room, turn on the TV for cloud noise, lay down on the floor, and try to sleep.

Once I woke up from my nap—I was fully engaged doing my mom role. I was checking homework, making dinner, planning parties, singing in the Church choir, calling my non-police friends, going bowling (in 2008 I married the man who recruited me to the A-Team bowling team 20 years earlier), cleaning, keeping up with extended family, giving medical care to my son, and supporting my children's goals.

Because I held being a mother as equal to being a cop—I was never seduced by the corrosive cop culture that slowly eats away at the morality of so many officers.

I genuinely did not have time to go out for a beer or to an officers-only (no kids or spouses invited) barbeque.

(Kevin 8, Calvin 7, Tawana 5)

During my career, I dealt with all the challenges that I outlined earlier and I saw a lot of the underside of life. But I also experienced compassion, generosity, and fellow feeling within

281

the department. Two things particularly come to mind. In 2000, my oldest son had to be hospitalized for four months due to complications from his muscular dystrophy. The Chief worked with me on that—making sure that I could balance my role as a cop and my role as a mom. My son lived four more years and died at the age of 32 in 2004.

My other son was in and out of corrections—which took a lot of emotional support on my end. However, he finally figured it out in his 30s. He's a father, has a decent job, and he's making me proud.

Just a testament as to how tenacious I was as a mother— when my daughter was in school—I never missed a single one of her basketball games in all four years. Now that took commitment! I couldn't stay for the whole game, but because her school was on my beat, I could radio the dispatcher and say, "I'm holding out for a minute" and get to part of every game.

When I look at it now, I see that having a very demanding career counterbalanced by a very committed home life—was the secret to my success on both fronts. My non-police friends, family, and activities kept me well rounded as opposed to the narrow mindedness and cynicism that takes its toll on too many career officers.

In 2007, I retired early from the now mergered Savannah-Chatham Metropolitan Police Department. There had been much corruption since the arrest of Anthony and the 11. I knew it was still corrupt, but I didn't know "who" I had to watch out for. So, like many other County officers, I opted for early retirement.

I thought back to the Corrections Office administrator who said, "I don't think you have what it takes to make a good officer."

As I transitioned from a Corrections Officer to a Police Officer—that same administrator told me, "You were a good officer." I knew it in my heart, but it was nice to hear it from the agency. Now, as a retired officer, I work part-time with the Chatham County Sheriff's Department in the Court House. I'm not done yet! I'm still serving and protecting.

Both Side of the Bars

Fifty One

The Road Ahead

"Knock, knock, knock, knock, knock, knock." This time, it's not the FBI coming to arrest me. This time, it's a call to action.

Though the knocking jolts me just as deeply as the morning of September 10, 1997, it's not paralyzing. It's invigorating.

Everything I've seen, everything I've learned—on both sides of the bars—is driving me forward. If I don't tell the secrets I've learned—about police, prisons, and personal choices—when I die, my hard-earned treasure will be buried with me.

My Mission

My mission is to share my lessons with as many people as possible. I started doing this when I was still behind bars. Fellow inmates were encouraged and inspired to reach higher.

Then, in 2008, when I was released—I immediately started helping my roommates in the Alston Wilkes Federal Halfway House. As soon as I was on my feet, I sought out volunteer opportunities with the homeless, teens at the Youth Detention Center, churches, prisons, schools, and law enforcement agencies.

Focus

Now, it's time to answer the "knock" in a bigger way. With the media spotlight fixed on the current challenges of police work—questioning excessive force and split second decisions—I'm reaching out to police departments for training. This is more than ethics training or choices based on our guiding principles. This training delivers proven methods to navigate cop culture, while keeping our families and personal lives intact.

At the same time, the community needs to be educated on the true demands it places on its officers. If the community wants to help, it needs to see the big picture—the bright side and the dark side—of law enforcement.

Writing this book was my first step to accelerate the education of the community and law enforcement. However, you can take a step too. If you found the message in this book to be valuable—please pass it forward. Also, the next time you see an officer, commend him or her for the service given to YOUR community. Ask officers about their families. Ask them about their challenges. Ask them what YOU can do to help.

About the Author

Anthony Bryant was a fun-loving, squeaky-clean kid who was determined to make a positive impact in his Savannah, Georgia community.

Though born into poverty, he thrived under the positive influence of his family, his five best basketball buddies, and his Westlake Avenue subsidized apartments neighborhood.

Anthony managed to escape the snares of drugs, underage drinking, and gangs. He grew up fast. Before his 20th birthday, he became a daddy, a husband, and an enlisted man serving as a communications expert in the US Army.

Six years later, he took a job as a Corrections Officer with the Chatham County Sheriff's Department, caring for inmates. Three years after that, he landed his "dream job"—and was sworn in as Officer Anthony Bryant with the Chatham County

Police Department. He prided himself in keeping the streets safe by putting criminals behind bars.

However, within two years this rock solid and fun loving family man succumbed to peer pressure within the police department, which ultimately shattered his life. Officer Anthony Bryant went from cop to criminal and landed on the other side of the bars.

Stripped of everything he cherished—Anthony hit rock bottom before surfacing 10 years later with a new understanding, a new hope, and a new mission for sharing the life-altering lessons he learned on both sides of the bars.

A man of faith, Anthony is soon to graduate from Northwest Nazarene University with a degree in Christian Family Ministry. Anthony speaks on ethics, cop culture, and leadership to law enforcement agencies, universities, and corporations. Additionally, Anthony speaks at schools and youth events and parent groups on Making Right Choices and Split-Second Decisions that Alter the Course of Your life.

Contact Anthony Bryant at
www.split2nd.weebly.com
Telephone: 803.521.9809

About the Co-Author

As I came to know Anthony, he reminded me that all of us are vulnerable.

Little compromises—unchecked—can lead to disaster. And yet, disaster doesn't have to be our final chapter. Anthony is living proof of a life reclaimed.—Patty Jo Sawvel

Originally, Anthony Bryant hired Patty Jo Sawvel to edit and publish his 20 page book. It became the wonderful framework for the book we have today. After, sharing in dozens of Skype interviews across state lines, pouring over court documents, and reviewing newspaper stories—we ended up with the treasure called *Both Sides of the Bars.*

During the process, Anthony often said, "Patty Jo, I forgot all about that. You are pulling things out of me that I haven't thought about in years." Of course, all of that "stuff" was what readers want to know—the why, the how, and the what.

Award-winning writer Patty Jo Sawvel has been recognized twice by the North Carolina Press Association for her work as an investigative reporter. Her book *Under the Influence: The Town That Listened to Its Kids* won the 2014 Global Ebook Award's Gold Medal in the non-fiction current events category.

Recently co-authored books include, *Bored to Death—5 Steps to Gear-Up & Be About THAT LIFE* by Henry Flowers and *Sharecropper's Wisdom: Growing Today's Leaders the Old Fashioned Way* by General J. R. Gorham. *Sharecropper's* won the 2016 Global Ebook Award's Silver Medal in the inspirational/visionary category.

Services—by Patty Jo Sawvel and Classic Writing—include interviewing, co-authoring (transforming interviews into a published book), editing, layout and design, and publishing.

For more information, visit www.ClassicWritingPR.com or call 336.906.7238.

Made in the USA
Columbia, SC
04 August 2020